DISNEY
PIRATES of the CARIBBEAN

THE COMPLETE VISUAL GUIDE

BY RICHARD PLATT AND GLENN DAKIN

Contents

Foreword
by Jerry Bruckheimer

I was young, in love with movies, and my eyes were glued to the screen, mesmerized, watching the daring, exciting, funny and acrobatic exploits of The Crimson Pirate, played by the great Burt Lancaster. Freewheeling, rebellious, unafraid to defy authority at every turn, the wind at your back and your ship pointed directly toward the freedom of the seven seas... what could be more fun than being a pirate... or at least being a pirate in the movies? I certainly had my favourite pirate films as a kid, including *Captain Blood*, *The Black Pirate*, and *Treasure Island*, all of them classics of swashbuckling and skullduggery.

And then, suddenly, as the world moved towards a new century, pirate movies went away. Vanished. Nobody cared any more, the skull and crossbones disappeared from the big screen. In a world of high-speed and hip-hop, the adventures of 18th century buccaneers had lost their relevancy... or had they?

At Disneyland in Anaheim, California, as well as other Disney parks around the world, the mid-1960s attraction known as 'Pirates of the Caribbean' had been drawing throngs since its opening, first as a miraculous leap of technology, and then as a nostalgic ride through the memories of grown-ups, and the imagination of their children. And when Walt Disney Studios asked me to find a way to translate the fun ride into a two-hour-plus feature film extravaganza, nothing could have excited me more. My dream of making a motion picture about pirates was about to come true. And the popularity of the movie that finally emerged in 2003, *Pirates of the Caribbean: The Curse of the Black Pearl*, not only fulfilled my hopes, but exceeded them. And thankfully, audiences around the world seemed to agree that we had not only breathed new life into a dead genre, but had actually reinvented it.

We wanted to take the pirate genre to a new level, one that had all the thrills and romance that you would expect from a big adventure, but with imaginative, unforgettable characters, state-of-the-art visual effects and a tip of the hat to the original Disneyland attraction, while taking off in whole new directions. Our director, Gore Verbinski, has a wonderful sense of humour and great storytelling skills. His enthusiasm is like a little kid's. He loves to work with actors, and actors love him. He was the perfect director for the project. As writers, we brought in the team of Ted Elliott and Terry Rossio – two wonderful writers who created a big hit with *Shrek* – to put our stamp on a draft by Jay Wolpert and Stuart Beattie which Disney first handed over to us. Ted and Terry brought in the element of the supernatural laced with lots of humour, which gave the story an edge that really interested me.

Then we had our stars, and it soon became clear after the film was released that Johnny Depp had created a brand new, authentic motion picture icon with his performance as Captain Jack Sparrow. Johnny's known for creating his own characters, and he had a definite vision for Jack Sparrow which was completely unique. We just let him go and he came up with this off-centre, yet very shrewd pirate, with his dreadlocks, gold teeth and grand assortment of ornamental beads and charms. He can't quite hold his balance, his speech is a bit slurred, so you assume he's either drunk, seasick or he's been on a ship too long. But it's all an act perpetrated for effect. And strange as it seems, it's also part of Captain Jack's charm. The Academy of Motion Picture Arts and Sciences certainly thought so, honouring Johnny with an Oscar nomination for Best Actor. We cast Orlando Bloom as Will Turner after he appeared in another of my productions, *Black Hawk Down*. I knew Orlando's time would come. I just didn't know how lucky we'd be to grab him before all the frenzy started with the *Lord of the Rings* films. We considered many young actresses for the role of Elizabeth Swann, but beauty alone was not enough. With Keira Knightley, who was then 17-years-old, we found beauty, brains and boldness, a great combination.

Millions of people from 8 to 80 took the ride with us, and clearly, they wanted more. So we created *Pirates of the Caribbean: Dead Man's Chest* and now *Pirates of the Caribbean: At World's End*, reuniting nearly the whole gang from the first film, with several exciting new additions as well. Gore is back, as are Ted and Terry, and of course Johnny, Orlando, Keira and much of the supporting cast. But we weren't interested in just doing a re-tread. Instead, everything in the first film gets pushed forward in *Dead Man's Chest*, and is pushed even further in *At World's End*. We love these characters and want to see what happens with them, deepening the characterizations and continuing the story. Much of the backdrop of *Dead Man's Chest* and *At World's End* is based on pirate lore, and the mythology of the seven seas, using elements of 18th century British history as a springboard. We have an astonishing new villain with Davy Jones, who along with his crew is unlike anything that's been seen before, as well as the power-mad English aristocrat Lord Cutler Beckett of the East India Trading Company.

Our production designer, an amazing creative individual named Rick Heinrichs, has added so many wonderful nuances to *Dead Man's Chest*, including epic-sized sets, a re-designed and re-built the *Black Pearl*, and *Flying Dutchman*, Davy Jones' fantastic mystery ship. And we've filmed, appropriate to our films' title, in some of the most exotic locations in all the Caribbean, including the rugged tropical paradise islands of Dominica and St. Vincent, and on the islands and turquoise oceans of the Bahamas.

This new DK book is a wonderful entry into the world of *Pirates of the Caribbean: The Curse of the Black Pearl*, *Dead Man's Chest* and *At World's End*, filled with pictures, illustrations and loaded with information about all three films. Like the original Disneyland 'Pirates of the Caribbean', we've tried to make our movies an "E" ticket attraction which everyone can ride together. So step aboard, mates, and sail off with us once again under the flag of adventure and imagination as limitless as the sea that stretches all the way to the far horizon. Keelhauling and walking the plank are definitely forbidden on this voyage!

Jerry Bruckheimer

Introduction

Behold – the Caribbean lies before you – a sight to enchant the eye of any adventurer. But no map can prepare you for the reality of a place which is more than half fantasy. No chart can mark the place where hopes end and nightmares begin. Do those faded lines denote a lost island, or perhaps a sleeping Kraken? Do those forbidding waters offer only death, or a way back from the World's End? There is a world of ghouls, goddesses and cursed gold that haunts the edges of the mundane realm we know. Only the brave or the foolhardy venture into this world of piracy and peril. You have your bearing – set sail and remember: take what you can – and give nothing back!

Caribbean

ISLANDS OF THE CARIBBEAN

Atlantic Ocean

Sea

The Pirata Codex

Set forth by Morgan and Bartholomew at the dawn of the great age of piracy, the *Pirata Codex* or Pirate Code is a revered collection of 'guidelines' that helps pirates to solve disputes without resorting to slaughter. One key entitlement preserved in its pages is the right to Parlay, which has enabled many a plunderer to blag his way to freedom instead of taking a short walk off of a shorter plank. Generally passed on by word of mouth, the Pirate Code book is rarely consulted as not many pirates can read anyway.

THE GREAT BOOK
The original codex – the handwritten volume of yellowing pages on which the words of Morgan and Bartholomew are preserved – is kept with Captain Teague. It can only be produced at the demand of a Pirate Lord.

In the Care of Captain Teague

The Keeper of the Code – non other than the man reputed to be Jack Sparrow's father, Captain Teague – keeps the book padlocked and Prison Dog carries the key. Teague insists that the Code is the law, and he will shoot anyone who speaks against it. However, deep down he knows that the real code is in a pirate's heart and comes down to one thing: what a man can do, and what a man can't do.

The Right of Parlay

One of the most important guidelines in the Code is the Right of Parlay. Parlay, coming from the French word parler – to speak – is a right granted to all pirates, enabling them to carry a vital message directly and in person to the very enemy commander who threatens their life.

UNDER PARLAY
Once the Right of Parlay has been invoked, the captive cannot be killed, tortured or relieved of any part of their anatomy until they have had their say. This is a very unpopular rule with pirates – until the tables are turned and they find themselves in need of it.

MISUNDERSTANDINGS ABOUT PARLAY
Honest folk unfortunate enough to stand in the way of pirate business may be disappointed if they invoke Parlay to delay their deaths. Sadly, you must be a pirate for the Code to apply. As Barbossa says, the Code is only a guideline.

How to Maroon a Man

The Code even provides guidelines on how marooning ought to be done. Finding a suitable island is extremely important. The island should be isolated, must be outside the Trade Winds, and preferably uncharted. Any man marooned on the island is to be given a gun, one shot and enough dry powder to end his misery.

The code is a broad document, even incorporating useful recipes – rum-based, of course.

To make a Heavy-Bodied Rum fit for a Marine at Sea: that needs to take One and one-half King's Gallon of Molasses for each gallon of rum that be desyrd.

Inkspots created by attempt at fancy calligraphy. Pirates believe the more ornate the writing is, the more binding it is.

first spoils to be divided = French Rules of Plunder

ARTYCLE II, SECTION I, PARAGRAPH VIII
This part of the Code is of special interest as it stipulates the sharing of the spoils. It opens by optimistically stating that the captain, in times of 'salutary fortune', can increase the share he allows the crew.

ARTYCLE II, SECTION II, PARAGRAPH I
Whoever first spots a treasure-laden ship can choose the best pistol found aboard for themselves. Amendations state that the rule applies only if the captain, the Master-At-Arms or the Quarter Master don't want the pistol.

§ VIII. Captaine may, in times of Salutary Fortune increase ye share of Alle, or of One, depending on Particular Circumstance, but he AND ye MASTER shalle not Fatten His Owne Purse with-out a Vote by ye Shipp's Companie.

§§ Section ye 2th

§ I. ye manne that 1st syghts a Sail of a Treasure-laden Shippe hath ye honour of choosing for himself ye best Pistol or Small Arme aboard ye Captured Vessel.

§ Beit Amended: Unless ye Captaine has a Preference for Said Weapon.

§ Beit Amended: Or ye Shippe's Master-At-Arms. *or Quarter Master*

§ II. ye Companie will Divvy up ye Spoyles of any seizure as follows

...to such large Items as Shippes, Dinghys... ...Vote, whenever Possible, or as be... ...ter.

...e's Senior Manne... ...pe's 2d-most Senior, Qt... ...ding above shall be... ...ye abovementioned... ...at Arms.

...es from Captured Goods. ...nterests of Shippe's ...Shippe's Companie ...s of Clothing that will ...ic clean Stockings. *without ridicule from the Cook*

...Rancid & malodorous ...come rades refuses to accept ...s Companie by Popular Vote, may Compel, ...d Threadbare Attire & Shift into Apparel ...arale Health & Good Morale.

Bloodsoaked garter used as bookmark

Amends relate to special cases governing piracy in the South China Seas.

Jack Sparrow

Born on a pirate ship in a typhoon, Captain Jack Sparrow has sea-water in his veins. At least, that's what his friends say. His enemies don't care whether his heart pumps blood, water or rum. They just want to see him at the end of a hangman's rope, or at the bottom of the sea. But Jack has an uncanny knack of escaping their clutches. Through bravery, luck and cunning, he manages to slip out of the tightest fixes.

The beads and trinkets in Jack's hair have been gathered from all over the world. Each one reminds him of a different adventure.

Hard to Starboard!

Jack is happiest at the helm of the *Black Pearl*. For him it is much more than "a keel; a hull; a deck and sails..." – it's freedom. Though his crew mutinied, he will always be Captain Jack Sparrow, and the *Pearl* will always be his.

TATTOOED AND BRANDED
Below the blue tattoo of a sparrow on Jack's right arm is a faint 'P' – proof that he has been accused of piracy, and was branded with a red-hot iron.

Hard-wearing linen trousers

Elizabeth's Choker

Jack seems like a desperate pirate who lets nothing stand between him and freedom or treasure. But he's not all bad. His threat to choke Elizabeth with the manacles that bind his hands is a bluff. After all, how could he kill a pretty woman whom he has just saved from a watery grave?

Dressed to Kill

There's a touch of the dandy about Jack, and his outfit shows off his status as captain. Long trousers, sea boots and knotted sash set him apart from his motley crew.

A Hit with the Ladies!

Jack's wit, charm and generous spirit make him popular company. So popular, in fact, that he has trouble remembering names and faces. The ladies in the taverns of Tortuga haven't forgotten Jack though, and they all think a slap or two will improve his memory.

Bottle stands upright on a pitching ship

Yo Ho Ho and a Bottle of Rum

Drinking is one of the most popular of pirate pleasures. Like all pirates, Jack believes that "rum gets you through times of no money better than money gets you through times of no rum."

When there's trouble on board, Jack's sword is rarely in its scabbard.

King of Thieves

Jack loves gold. On *Isla de Muerta* he drapes himself with treasure. With pearls around his neck and rings on his fingers, a finishing touch is a jewel-encrusted gold crown.

Sneaky Jack

Captain Jack's silver tongue helps him to weasel his way past the most alert sentries – at least for a while. To get on board the *Interceptor*, he tells its guards that the *Black Pearl* can outsail any other ship. While they argue about whether or not the *Pearl* and its crew of cursed sailors even exists, Jack slips onto the deck.

No Escape?

When fine words don't work, trickery usually does. Surrounded by bayonets and almost certainly bound for the gallows, Jack takes Elizabeth hostage. A handy crane hoists him quickly out of harm's way, and he slides down a rope to make good his escape.

Pirate Possessions

Jack has few worldly goods to his name – they are all too easily stolen, gambled away or lost overboard – but what he does have he holds dear. His grandest possession is his ship, the *Black Pearl*, whilst smaller items, like his hat, have sentimental value. Weapons are the tools of a pirate's trade, so Jack never likes to lend or borrow them. An unusual compass is the most special of all his things. He consults it constantly and is wary about giving his most trusted shipmates even a glance at its gently spinning dial.

Lid shows map of the heavens

Central shadow vane makes compass work as a sundial

Compass disc sliced from a walrus tusk

Magnetic Marvel

Although it appears to be useless (the needle never points to the north), Jack's compass has supernatural qualities. The compass cannot be used to navigate in a conventional sense, but it does direct the owner to whatever he or she most desires. Jack acquired the compass from a voodoo priestess named Tia Dalma seven years earlier.

Domed cover made from pure lapis lazuli

Bone Paddle

Nobody escapes from a Turkish prison alive, so Jack sneaks inside a coffin to get out. The guards tip the dead prisoners from a cliff-top and the falling tide carries the caskets out to sea. Something stirs within one of the bobbing boxes. Jack Sparrow pops up and borrows a handy oar from his fellow passenger.

Rounded hip joint makes a comfortable hand-hold

Foot doubles as oar-blade

PULLING YOUR LEG
"Sorry mate," quips Jack as he wrenches a bony oar from a rotting hip. It lasts just long enough to paddle him as far as the *Black Pearl*. "If you ask right, there's always someone willing to give you a leg-up," he tells Gibbs.

Fighting Jack

Jack has become an expert buccaneer, defending himself with his trusty sword and pistol. An Italian fencing master taught him many of his sword skills – in exchange for a captured cargo of Chinese silk. Marksmanship took him a little longer to master. He trained himself to shoot by taking aim at empty wine bottles tossed from the *Pearl*'s deck rail. A bucket of shot and a sack of gunpowder later, he could hit nine out of ten bottles.

Cold Steel

Jack's sabre is longer than the cutlass that most pirates favour. For a pirate who's in trouble as much as Jack, it's important to keep his enemies a couple of extra inches away. Jack's battle with Barbossa on *Isla de Muerta* proves he made a sensible choice as he more than matches his arch-enemy blow for blow.

Hand-guard stops blood running down the blade and staining his sleeves

Jack keeps the cutting edge extremely sharp

Hot Powder

Jack cherishes his flintlock pistol, but he never pulls the trigger. He vowed not to fire the gun except in a fair fight with Barbossa. When Jack's treacherous first mate marooned him on a desert island, he gave Jack his pistol and just one shot – to kill himself. But Jack escaped, and nine years later he gets his revenge, shooting Barbossa on *Isla de Muerta*.

Decorative design inlaid in silver

Flint springs forward when the trigger is pulled, striking sparks to ignite gunpowder

Jack cleans and polishes the barrel daily to clean off the rust that forms quickly in the salty sea air

Thanks to its heavy pommel, gun doubles as a lethal club

Essential Hat

Any self-respecting pirate captain feels naked without his hat. Jack Sparrow is no exception. The black tricorn is battered and faded, but still serves him well. It's practical as well as decorative: he's filled it with cool fresh water to drink at wells and trapped deadly scorpions in its domed crown.

Faded leather has been scorched by Caribbean sun and beaten by harsh sea winds

Port Royal

Founded by the English, Port Royal is a bustling harbour town situated on the eastern tip of Jamaica. The town is built around Fort Charles, England's biggest government fort in the Caribbean. Or at least it was. A battering from the cannons of the *Black Pearl* leaves the fort quite a lot smaller – and boosts the pirates' power.

Docks and Castle

Towering over the town, Fort Charles is supposed to protect the ships of the Royal Navy moored in the harbour below. The cannons that point out from the battlements are a menacing warning to pirates cruising offshore. However, the fort's garrison is helpless when Jack and Will sneak on board the *Dauntless* and sail it out to sea.

HARBOURMASTER ON THE MAKE

With his wig, spectacles and tricorn hat, the Harbourmaster seems like a loyal servant of the king, but not everything is as it seems. Years of mixing with maritime riffraff have corrupted him. When Jack offers a small bribe to keep his arrival secret, the Harbourmaster cannot resist.

Bribes help the Harbourmaster to buy fine clothes he could not afford on his meagre government salary.

LIAR'S LOG

The Harbourmaster's ledger records the details of every ship and sailor tying up at the dock. Jack's handful of coins ensures that he doesn't appear in it.

GONE FISHING

It's not all business at Port Royal's wharf. There's always time to fit in a bit of angling. This ragged lad hopes to catch enough for dinner by the time the sun goes down.

Shopping Spree

Stretching back from the harbour, shops jostle for space with Port Royal's many taverns. Here an enterprising captain can find everything he needs, from tar for a ship's bottom to smuggled lace for his lady love.

As well as regular remedies, the apothecary mixes potions to mend a broken heart or to stop a dog from straying. When merchant ships dock, he's kept busy selling pox cures to the crew.

The Bit 'n' Stirrup *supplies bits, bridles and lots of other equipment for Port Royal's horses, including those from Fort Charles.*

S. GARRETT
CHYMIST & DRUGGIST

1704

With all the vessels dropping anchor at Port Royal there is a constant supply of sailors looking for a hearty meal and a bed for the night. Not all innkeepers welcome pirates but at the Whale and Waterspout, *old Mr Garrett turns a blind eye – as long as his guests pay their bill in full.*

Sweet Fruit and Sewers

Though Port Royal's street markets overflow with juicy tropical fruit, the air is far from sweet. The town doubled in size in 10 years, and the sewer system can't cope.

THAT SINKING FEELING

Captain Jack Sparrow makes an unusual yet graceful entrance to Port Royal harbour. He steps onto the wooden dock from the masthead of the purloined fishing trawler, the *Jolly Mon*. Jack makes port just in time – despite bailing as fast as he can, his craft silently sinks beneath him.

CONTRABAND CARGOES

Port Royal's customs officials are just as corrupt as the Harbourmaster. In exchange for a share of a ship's cargo, they turn their backs while smugglers land their goods – free of import duty. Then the smugglers load up with rum and sugar to smuggle back to America.

Governor Swann

Appointed by the King of England, Wetherby Swann is the proud Governor of the British colony at Port Royal on the vibrant and prosperous island of Jamaica. Undoubtedly Swann is charming and polite but it's no secret that he hasn't the skill to govern his rebellious daughter Elizabeth, let alone an entire island!

Though his wig makes his head hot and itchy, Swann feels undressed without it.

Loving Father

Since the death of his wife, Governor Swann has raised his daughter Elizabeth on her own. Over the years Elizabeth has blossomed into a beautiful young lady, although at times she drives her father to distraction with her wilfulness and disregard for propriety!

LIVING LIKE A LORD

Set in the fashionable St. Paul's district, Governor Swann's grand mansion is far from the squalor of Port Royal's docks and slums.

Luxurious ostrich feathers trim his tricorn hat

Aristocratic Attire

Ruling over a British colony demands a certain authority, and Governor Swann dresses to impress. His fashionable frock coat comes from his London tailor, and his cravat from Paris. It's a shame he does not pay as much attention to his work as he does to his appearance.

Under Attack

Swann's cosy world is turned upside down when the *Black Pearl* launches an attack on Port Royal. Lured by the Gold Medallion that Elizabeth wears around her neck, the pirates storm the governor's mansion. By the time the governor returns to his wrecked home, his daughter is sailing from the port, a captive of Barbossa.

FORT IN FLAMES

Towering over the docks, Fort Charles guards Port Royal from pirate attack. At least, that's the idea. In fact, the fort has too few cannons. Its soldiers are better at drill and parades than warfare. The garrison finds it hard to defend itself; protecting the people of Port Royal as well is impossible. Pirates rule the Caribbean, and their ships are heavily armed. As cannonballs batter the stone walls of the fort, the ramparts are no place for dithering Governor Swann, who quakes with fear at every blast.

Armless Fun

When Barbossa's crew swarms aboard the *Dauntless*, Swann cowers in the captain's quarters. He is soon discovered by a bloodthirsty pirate and only just escapes his grasp. But Swann's ordeal isn't over; to his horror, during their skirmish, the arm of his cursed assailant comes off and has a life all of its own.

"ELIZABETH, ARE YOU THERE?"

On board the *Dauntless* Swann orders Elizabeth to remain in the captain's quarters and out of harm's way. But he underestimates his daughter's spirit and determination and discovers that she has escaped using knotted bed sheets so she can help Will.

Elizabeth Swann

Hair elegantly
swept up

In fine silk clothes, Elizabeth Swann looks every
inch a lady. She plays the part of the perfect governor's daughter
but secretly Port Royal society bores her. She dreads the thought
of being a commodore's wife, respectable but dull. She dreams
instead of a life of adventure. She cannot forget the moment
eight years ago when she glimpsed a pirate ship on her voyage
from England. At once both thrilling and frightening, it stood
for everything she yearns for: excitement, danger and freedom!

*Delicate antique
lace trim*

Sailing for Port Royal

*Tightly-laced corset
beneath the dress
makes it hard for
Elizabeth to
breathe*

Much to her father's dismay,
pirates have always fascinated
Elizabeth. As a girl on the
voyage to Port Royal, she
sang their songs. When the
crew rescued a survivor from
a pirate attack, she recognised
the pirate Medallion he wore.

Wearing Aztec Gold

Elizabeth took the Medallion
from young Will Turner so that
the ship's crew would not guess
he was associated with pirates.
She has kept it hidden ever
since, but she doesn't realise
the trouble it will bring.

*A fan gives
slight relief
from the
tropical sun*

BREATHTAKING FASHIONS
Laced tightly into a corset and
fashionable dress, Elizabeth
feels suffocated. She's happier
disguised in sailors' clothes
that let her move easily.

Not Just a Pretty Face

Elizabeth is quick-witted and clever. When she goes aboard the *Black Pearl* to 'Parlay' with Barbossa, she uses the Gold Medallion to strike a bargain. Her threat to drop it overboard makes the captain cooperate, but she soon finds she was foolish to trust him. Barbossa sails away, with Elizabeth still on board.

On Board the Terror Ship

In Elizabeth's dreams of an adventurous life she did not imagine herself being tossed in the air by a crew of skeletons. After her terrifying chase around the moonlit deck of the *Black Pearl*, she cowers in a corner of Barbossa's cabin.

Preparing for Battle

A challenge brings out the best in Elizabeth. With the *Black Pearl* in hot pursuit of the *Interceptor*, most women of her time would have taken cover. Instead Elizabeth is in the thick of the fighting. She takes command, figures out a way to turn the ship, and shouts "Fire all!" to start the battle.

Love and Loyalty

Above all, Elizabeth follows her heart. Marriage to Commodore Norrington would have brought her wealth and respect. But she would rather wed a humble blacksmith and become Mrs Elizabeth Turner. Even her father realises that he cannot persuade Elizabeth to change her mind.

Smoke Signals

Marooned with Captain Jack on a desert island, Elizabeth is horrified to discover that this bold pirate has no idea how to escape. While Jack drinks himself senseless, she burns his stock of rum. The huge fire alerts the navy, and they are rescued the next morning.

Will Turner

Until he met Jack Sparrow, swordsmith Will Turner was a simple craftsman. His life revolved around his work, and his distant longing for a woman he knew could never be his wife. But in a few short hours his world is turned upside down. He finds himself sucked into a nightmarish world of pirates, ghouls, adventure and betrayal.

Will can throw axe with amazing precision

Man Overboard!

Will first met Elizabeth when they were children and he was rescued after pirates attacked the ship on which he was sailing. Told to care for the half-drowned boy, Elizabeth immediately felt drawn to him – although she was worried when she found a pirate Medallion round his neck.

Simple jerkin

Bootstrap fitted a chain to the Medallion so Will could wear it

MYSTERIOUS MEDALLION

Will believed his father was a respectable merchant seaman. When he sent Will an Aztec Medallion, his son thought it was just an exotic trinket that he had picked up on his travels. Will is shocked and dismayed when Jack reveals to him that his father was 'Bootstrap Bill' Turner, "a good man, and a good pirate".

Ominous skull

Made for Each Other

Eight years after they met, Will is the man of Elizabeth's dreams. However, she does not dare tell him how she feels, for her father would never let them marry. A governor's daughter is too good for a lowly blacksmith!

Leather shoes with silver buckles

Proud Craftsman

In this dusty Port Royal smithy Will pumps the huge bellows and stokes the charcoal furnace. The furnace flames heat cold steel until it glows white hot. Forging a beautiful sword blade is punishing work; the many hours of hammering, folding, grinding and polishing have given Will patience and strength.

ASLEEP ON THE JOB

Will's master is a man named John Brown. Although Brown is a drunk who seldom does any work, it is his forge and so his name decorates the swords Will makes. He takes the credit for catching Jack Sparrow too, after a lucky blow with an empty bottle.

Duel with a Pirate

Will is as handy with a blade as any soldier. He ought to be; after making the swords, he practises fencing with them for hours each day. When he discovers Jack in the forge, pirate captain and swordsmith are almost equally matched. "You know what you're doing, I'll give you that," quips Jack, who only manages to avoid losing to Will by acrobatic blade work – and old-fashioned cheating.

A LOYAL ALLY

When Jack faces the hangman, Will rushes to save his life – at great risk to his own. Though Will knows that he might be hanged as a pirate himself, he has a strong sense of what's right and what's not.

WILL'S SWORD

Unlike the ceremonial sword he made for Commodore Norrington's promotion, Will's weapon looks simple. It has a plain cast-iron grip, and a 'half-basket' hilt protects his hand. The blade is special, though. By using the methods of Spanish swordsmiths, Will has made it immensely strong, yet light and flexible.

Will proudly engraved his own name on this blade

Blade has double-edged point for cutting and thrusting

Norrington

Loyal service to his majesty the King of England has brought James Norrington respect and status. As captain of HMS *Interceptor*, he has chased and captured some of the Caribbean's most fearsome pirates. He is promoted from Captain to Commodore of the Fleet, an advance that brings Norrington some satisfaction, but he still lacks the one thing that can bring him true happiness – taking Elizabeth Swann as his wife.

HMS Interceptor

Norrington's ship, the *Interceptor*, is perfect for chasing pirates in Caribbean waters. She is a brig and carries guns on two decks. Thanks to her fine lines she is fast and can turn quickly but she's no match for the *Black Pearl*.

Loyal Officer

To maintain an air of authority, a captain in the English Navy cannot afford to show any emotion in front of his crew. Norrington has spent so many years masking his feelings that even in his personal affairs he is distant. Unfortunately for him, this is a trait that Elizabeth cannot bear.

MUDDLED MARINES
Red-coated marines guard Norrington's ships. Unfortunately, the bumbling Murtogg and Mullroy are more of a hindrance than a help.

GLEAMING STEEL
To mark his promotion, Norrington is given a new sword by Governor Swann. Beautifully hand-forged by Will Turner, it's perfectly balanced, and gold filigree decorates the handle.

On Parade

Norrington's promotion ceremony at the fort is a glittering military spectacle. Pipes and drums play. Sailors and marines march in perfect formation. Norrington himself is the star of the show. What better time to propose to Elizabeth? Unfortunately her corset spoils everything, and she plunges swooning from the battlements into the sea.

DEATH SENTENCE

Norrington does not let sentiment get in the way of duty. The punishment for piracy on the high seas is death. Jack has also committed many other crimes – including impersonating a cleric of the Church of England – so the sentence is clear. Jack Sparrow must hang.

Death warrant is drawn up and awaits Governor Swann's signature.

Dazzling and Desirable

The Commodore is sure that he loves Elizabeth, but there are other reasons for marrying her. She can introduce him to important London families. And when her wealthy father dies, Elizabeth will inherit a small fortune.

BEATEN IN LOVE...

When Elizabeth stands by Will in protecting Jack, Norrington knows his rival in love has beaten him. He accepts defeat nobly, telling Will "This is a beautiful sword. I would expect the man who made it to show the same care in every aspect of his life."

...AND IN LIFE

After Jack escapes from Port Royal, recapturing him becomes a mission that takes over Norrington. He chases the pirate all over the world, until he makes a fatal mistake. In pursuit of Jack he orders his crew to sail through a hurricane, wrecking his ship. He is dismissed from the navy for his foolishness, and becomes a penniless drunk.

Pirates Beware!

After his capture, Jack Sparrow is given lodgings looking out across Port Royal bay. Unfortunately prison bars rather spoil the view. It's not the first time Jack has been locked up, but he's worried, nonetheless. Imprisonment is the beginning of a story that soon ends, with "a short drop and a sudden stop", for the punishment for piracy is the hangman's noose. Inside Port Royal's prison, Jack thinks about this hazard, but he does not give up hope. After all, he has cheated the hangman before. Why should this time be different?

Jailer with a Tail

Jack takes one look at his doggy jailer and decides that he is no more likely to hand over the keys than a human guard. "The dog is never going to move," he tells his fellow prisoners as they try and lure the hound within reach with a bone.

"I Know Those Guns!"

The sound of gunfire makes Jack Sparrow spring from his hard stone seat to gaze at the bay. Although his prison cell is directly in the firing line, the blasts are music to his ears, for he quickly recognises the sound of the guns as those of his beloved *Black Pearl*.

BOUND FOR THE GALLOWS
Jack's criminal companions are desperate to avoid the hangman. Though they can't tempt the Prison Dog, a cannonball sets them free. As they escape though a hole in their cell wall they sympathise with Jack, still locked inside. "You've no manner of luck at all," they tell him.

THE TRYALS OF PIRATES, Viz.

Peter Marshall, James Kiley, after Killa, Courtney Anderson, Charles Stewart, James Robinson,

Ernest Lauterio, Scott Bailey, David Gordon, Mark Davies, Larry Dias

VOLUNTEERS

God Save the K...

Able SEAMEN OF OLD ENGLAND

Death Sentence

This time, Jack keeps his appointment with the hangman. Moments away from death, he can't help smiling as he remembers some of the crimes the town clerk reads out: "...impersonating a cleric of the Church of England... sailing under false colours... arson... depravity…". His smile fades as the list ends "...you are sentenced to be hung by the neck until dead...".

A Narrow Escape

Just as Jack is beginning to think that his luck has finally run out, Will dashes to the rescue. He draws his sword, and hurls it at the very moment that the hangman pulls the lever to execute Jack. By standing on Will's blade, Jack stops the noose from tightening round his neck.

PIRATES YE BE WARNED

A simple wooden sign accompanies the swaying bodies

A Gruesome Display

Commodore Norrington shows off the bodies of executed pirates near the quay. He hopes that this grisly spectacle will encourage passing sailors to obey the law. To preserve the corpses, they are lightly boiled in sea-water and dipped in tar before being put on display.

Black Pearl

With sails as dark as a moonless night, and a hull painted to match, the *Black Pearl* is every inch a pirate ship. She's built for action, too: behind the gunports on each side are two rows of deadly cannons. Sailing the *Pearl* demands teamwork, skill and strength. The crew work together to stretch the tattered sails tight against the gusty wind. When danger threatens, they'll fight to the death to defend themselves and their beloved ship.

Who's in Charge?

Pirate ships have captains, just as naval ships do, but pirates obey only the orders they agree with! Sailors on the *Pearl* vow to uphold the Pirate Code. But the rules it contains are more like guidelines: the crew can even change their captain if they don't like him.

NAVIGATION

Though Jack often lets his special compass guide him, he navigates just as other seamen do. Near coasts, he relies on charts (sea maps). Far from land, he uses an instrument called a sextant to measure the sun's height at noon. From this he can calculate how far he's sailed north or south.

Wooden tube makes the spyglass light and easy to handle

SPYGLASS

Spotting distant ships and shores at sea isn't easy – even from the crow's nest. So mariners use a spyglass (telescope) nicknamed the 'bring-em-closer' to magnify the view.

The Only Woman on Board

Like all mariners, pirates are a superstitious lot, and they believe that women on board a ship will always bring bad luck. They make one exception: wooden women are allowed, but only if they are nailed to the bow as a figurehead. The *Black Pearl's* figurehead shows a beautiful woman with an outstretched arm and a bird about to take flight from her hand.

There are no flush lavatories on a pirate ship! Instead the crew takes advantage of the 'seats of ease' – holes in the deck behind the figurehead, with seats fixed above.

Mariners believe the eyes of the figurehead help their ship to find its way at sea

LOADING FOOD
Fresh food is a luxury on the *Pearl* because it soon rots in the tropical heat. Mostly the crew live on hard tack (biscuits), and salted meat. The captain eats better and the ship carries a few live sheep and chickens for his table.

SHIP'S SUPPLIES
To load supplies into the hold at the very bottom of the ship, the crew lower them down a hatchway. For heavier supplies they use the yards as cranes.

NIGHTY-NIGHT SHIPMATES!
The *Pearl's* crew sleep on deck, or in hammocks below when the weather is bad. With the gunports closed, there is little ventilation, and the air at night quickly turns foul. Sailors wake with a horrid taste in their mouths as though they have been sucking a penny.

Life Below Deck

The *Black Pearl* is like the world in miniature, made out of wood, rope, tar, and canvas. When its crew set off on a voyage of piracy, they must take with them absolutely everything they will need until their next landfall. So, deep down in the hold you'll find not only supplies of food and water, but also extra sails and ropes, and spare lumber for making repairs to the ship. There's enough gunpowder and ammunition to start a small war, and even a chest of drugs and surgeon's instruments to treat the wounded.

High above the deck, the ragged sails are misleading: blown along on a supernatural breeze, the *Pearl* can outsail any ship in the Caribbean.

Jolly Roger flag flies from the top of the main mast, the highest point of the ship. To victims it signals that the Pearl's crew shows no mercy, and expects none in return. Every pirate ship flies a trademark variation on the skull-and-crossbones theme: cutlasses support the Pearl's grinning death's head.

From the crow's nest, a lookout can see enemy ships twice as far away as a sailor can from the deck far below.

Between the ropes that support the mast are ratlines — rope rungs that form a ladder leading up to the yard-arms. The crew climbs them barefoot to adjust the sails, often in gales or in total darkness.

Raising the huge anchor is a job for the whole crew. Its thick cable (rope) is as wide as a man's leg, and is immensely heavy.

The galley where food is cooked is just in front of the foremast. During rough weather the cook douses the stove to reduce the risk of a fire. The crew has to make do with cold food until the sea is calmer.

Below decks the Pearl is dark, dingy, and stuffy. Gratings covering the hatchway let in some air, but the ship's boats on top block out much of the light. In bad weather tarpaulin covers seal the hatchway completely, making the lower deck gloomier still.

The bilges at the very bottom of the ship stink. Everything liquid drains here from the upper decks, and in bad weather crew members sometimes use them as a lavatory.

Every day the crew has to swab the decks. This mopping stops the planks from drying, shrinking and springing leaks.

During the day the crewmen roll up their hammocks and stow them around the upper deck – where they protect against gunfire in battle.

Firing a cannon is easy: the crew just touches a glowing taper to a trail of gunpowder. The tricky part is reloading. It takes five sailors five minutes to clean the gun, damp down sparks, then ram powder, ball, and wadding down the barrel.

At the stern, beneath the quarterdeck, the Great Cabin is the most comfortable place on the ship. Most of the time it's the captain's private cabin, but in a battle the furniture folds neatly away, and the cabin becomes a gundeck.

The captain commands the ship from quarterdeck at the stern.

Whale oil burning in lanterns at the stern helps the ship avoid collision during the night. Dousing them for an attack makes the ship almost invisible.

Barbossa

Ruthless and cunning, Barbossa has one aim: to become mortal once more. He leads his crew in search of gold and blood to lift the Aztec curse. Without them, Barbossa cannot die – but can never truly live. It is a punishment he deserves, for Barbossa rose through the ranks, and through treachery and cruelty he swiftly became captain. Barbossa signed on as first mate on the *Black Pearl*. The mutiny he led robbed Captain Jack Sparrow of his ship.

Blue ostrich feathers show Barbossa's vanity

Grudge Match

Barbossa marooned the overthrown captain, Jack Sparrow, on a desert island. Barbossa gave Jack a gun with just one shot – to kill himself when heat and thirst got too much. So Barbossa is amazed when Jack reappears.

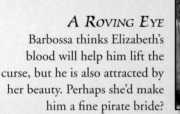

A ROVING EYE
Barbossa thinks Elizabeth's blood will help him lift the curse, but he is also attracted by her beauty. Perhaps she'd make him a fine pirate bride?

No Mercy!

Once Barbossa realises that it is Will's blood he really needs, Elizabeth is worthless to him. He doesn't hesitate to make her walk the plank, to face the sharks – or a slower death on a barren island.

Buttons made from melted down Inca silver stolen from Spanish ships

Old but Powerful

Barbossa is old enough to be the father of some members of his crew, but none question his authority. Even when they blame him for the Aztec curse, Barbossa's legendary skill with a sword makes sure he remains their chief.

BARBOSSA'S RING

Plundered from a Venetian ship, Barbossa's ring shows a lion's head – the symbol of a leader.

Flesh to Bones

As Barbossa steps from his cabin onto the moonlit deck, Elizabeth at last sees him as the phantom that he really is. "You'd best start believing in ghost stories, Miss Turner..." the living corpse tells her "...you're in one!"

The Cursed Crew

Scoundrels, murderers and malefactors, drunkards and desperadoes sail the *Black Pearl*. In other words, the ship has a crew of perfectly ordinary pirates. Or they would be ordinary, if they were not cursed like their captain. To end the curse, they will follow Barbossa anywhere. Their quest has taken them so long that – like the sails – their clothes are in tatters, and salt crusts their hair. With their attack on Port Royal, the pirates sense that they will soon be leaving the world of the living dead. For the last Gold piece and the blood of 'Bootstrap Bill' are almost within reach.

Pintel practises his famous scowl in front of a mirror

All Hands on Deck!

The members of the *Black Pearl*'s crew come from a dozen nations, and include escaped slaves from West Africa and Hispaniola. Most were once privateers – sailors who plundered enemy vessels during wartime. When peace returned, they lost their jobs and were lured into piracy.

Washing clothes in chamberlye (urine) after a battle gets out the worst of the blood stains

MONKEY BUSINESS
The smallest member of the crew is also one of the most useful. Named 'Jack' after Jack Sparrow, Barbossa's pet monkey takes care of the precious Gold Medallion. He carries it far out of reach in the rigging when danger threatens.

Fashionable large-buckled leather shoe

Dim-witted Duo

Pintel and Ragetti are cutthroat pirates but more often than not their lack of common sense and their constant bickering make them the clowns of Barbossa's crew. They were press-ganged by the English Navy, but jumped ship after a year of beatings, bad food and boredom, and eventually found themselves onboard the *Black Pearl*.

Ragetti lost his eye in battle. The wooden replacement given to him by Barbossa "splinters somefink terrible."

Jacket stolen from a French nobleman

DEVIOUS DISGUISES

It is Pintel and Ragetti that Barbossa chooses to create a diversion while the rest of the crew walk out to the *Dauntless*: "This is just like what the Greeks done at Troy... 'cept they was in a horse, 'stead of dresses."

SWARMING ABOARD

The *Pearl's* crew meet fierce resistance as they swing across to the *Interceptor*. They are not used to such opposition. Crews attacked by pirates – even flesh-and-blood pirates – usually give in without a battle.

Explosive!

Home-made grenades help to spread panic and confusion during the pirates' attacks. The bombs are made from pottery globes stuffed with gunpowder and explode with lots of smoke and noise.

Caked-on tar gives trousers extra water resistance – and a pungent odour

FIRING A BROADSIDE

Barbossa waits until the *Interceptor* is alongside before ordering the crew to fire. Cannons are not accurate enough to hit distant targets, and like most pirates, the *Pearl's* crew is too disorganised to make good use of them.

Curse of the Aztec Gold

Doomed by their greed, the *Black Pearl*'s cursed crew regrets the day it found the Gold. At first the men laughed at stories that it was cursed. They could believe that Hernando Cortés, the Spanish conquistador, had once owned it. Maybe it was true that Mexico's Aztec rulers used it to bribe Cortés, to stop him looting their country. But the curse? "Ridiculous superstition!", said Barbossa. Alas, he was wrong, and by the time he learned the truth, it was too late.

Phantom Captain

When Barbossa steps into the moonlight, the grim effects of the curse are plain to see. The flesh vanishes from his bones, and he becomes a walking skeleton. To lift the curse, Barbossa must return every piece of Aztec Gold to the stone chest from which it came – and add the blood of 'Bootstrap Bill'.

Rotting flesh hangs from bleached white rib bones

Moonlight turns Barbossa's fine clothes to rags

APPLE AGONY

Barbossa and his crew suffer a living death, feeling and tasting nothing: "...drink would not satisfy; food turned to ash in our mouths." The pirate captain is tormented by flavourless apples. He longs to be mortal, so that he can once more taste the flesh of the fruit, and feel the juice running down his chin.

Cursed Crew

Pintel and Ragetti are cursed like the others, wandering the world as skeletons that cannot be killed. Their longing to lift the curse has given them a sixth sense, that lures them to the Gold pieces. "The Gold calls to us," they tell Elizabeth as they find her with the Aztec Medallion in the governor's house.

A Surprise for Jack

Jack Sparrow had heard rumours that the treasure was cursed, but (luckily for him) his crew marooned him before he could take his share of the Gold. He learns the truth when one of the mutinous crew grabs him through the bars of Port Royal prison. As moonlight falls on the pirates arm, Jack mutters "So there is a curse. That's interesting."

Treasure Chest

The Aztecs placed 882 identical pieces of gold in a stone chest which they gave to Cortés, "blood money paid to stem the slaughter he wreaked upon them with his armies". Instead of satisfying him, the gold merely fuelled his greed, so the heathen gods placed a curse upon the gold: any mortal that removes a piece from the chest shall be damned.

DEEP SEA DESPERADOES

Sometimes the curse has advantages. The pirates are indestructible phantoms and don't float in sea-water, the way mortals do. So to stage a surprise attack on the *Dauntless*, moored in the shallows off the coast of *Isla de Muerta*, they simply walk upon the sea bed and climb up the ship's anchor.

JACK'S PLAN

Jack shrewdly uses the curse to get his revenge. By secretly palming a coin he becomes immortal. Then, when Barbossa's men are aboard the *Dauntless*, he shoots their captain – just as Will drops the last coin, and his own blood, into the chest. Human once more, Barbossa dies.

A TABLE OF TREATS

On board the *Black Pearl*, the pirates look forward to becoming human again. Like Barbossa, they long to taste food once more, and fantasise about what they will eat first when the curse is lifted.

A Motley Crew

Of all the pirate islands in the Caribbean, none is the equal of Tortuga. Dangerous, boisterous, drunken and bawdy, Tortuga is pirate heaven. So it's no surprise that when Captain Jack Sparrow is looking for a crew, he steers a course here. Named by the Spanish after the turtle it resembles, the island lies to the north of Hispaniola. It is far enough from civilisation to escape attention, but conveniently close to the route the treasure-ships sail. Surely Jack will find men mad enough to join him on his dangerous adventure here.

A Worthy First Mate

Jack quickly finds a loyal first mate, sleeping in a pig-sty. Joshamee Gibbs is an old friend of Jack's. He served in the Royal Navy for a while but Jack forgave him for this because he deserted his post and turned pirate once more.

JACK'S LEVERAGE

Will thinks that Jack is leading him to Elizabeth because he freed Jack from jail, and because he knew his father. However, when Will hears Jack refer to him as his 'leverage', he begins to suspect that he only knows half the story.

RELUCTANT PIRATE

The crew member with the least experience of all is Will himself. For a blacksmith however, he turns out to be a pretty good sailor. Once he gets over his sea-sickness, he learns to scamper up the rigging as nimbly as any midshipman. Jack is not surprised; he knows that with 'Bootstrap Bill' for a father, Will has piracy in his blood.

Crew on Parade

"Feast your eyes, Captain! All of them faithful hands before the mast...", Gibbs tells Jack as he parades the crew. Will doubts their skill, but Jack doesn't mind. He knows that sailors have to be either mad or stupid to sign up for the kind of mission he has in mind.

Speechless

Cotton doesn't reply when Jack asks him whether he has the courage and fortitude to join the crew – he can't because his tongue has been cut out. "Wind in your sails!" Cotton's parrot replies for him. "We figure that means 'Yes'," explains Gibbs.

Angry Anamaria

At the end of the line a crew member with a large hat asks in a suspiciously high-pitched voice "What's the benefit for us?" It's Anamaria, and she believes that Jack has a debt to repay. "You stole my boat!" she accuses him, adding a couple of slaps for emphasis. Jack admits he deserves them, but he can hardly return the *Jolly Mon* now. After all, it's sitting at the bottom of Port Royal harbour.

Stormy Weather

The crew face their first test when a ferocious storm hits the ship. Despite striking all but the mainsail, the *Interceptor* is swamped by the mountainous waves. United by danger, the crew battle with the storm and survive.

The Crew See Action

When the *Black Pearl* starts to chase the *Interceptor*, Jack's crew really show what they can do. Despite never having sailed before, Elizabeth comes up with some ideas to help them gain speed and win vital minutes to prepare for battle. But once they have thrown all the cannonballs overboard, what are they going to fire from the guns? "Case-shot and langrage! Nails and crushed glass!" orders Gibbs. When they open fire on the *Black Pearl*, Ragetti is the first to taste this strange ammunition – a fork hits his wooden eye.

Taking the Lead

Elizabeth discovers to her dismay that the crew really do follow the pirate code of "he who falls behind gets left behind." They won't follow her to *Isla de Muerta* to rescue Will. All she can do is to launch the boat herself and row back alone.

Isla de Muerta

What better place to hide treasure than an island that cannot be found – except by those who know where it is? *Isla de Muerta*, or 'Island of the Dead', is just such a place. It was to here that Barbossa sailed using the bearings he had tricked from Jack Sparrow. It was in the echoing cave here on the island that Barbossa found the stone chest of Aztec Gold. And it's to the same stone chest that the crew of the *Black Pearl* returns the 882 pieces of Aztec Gold as it finds them, one by one.

Strange Kind of Treasure

The pirates don't just bring the Aztec Gold to *Isla de Muerta*. They heap up all their plunder in the cave. Until the curse is lifted wealth is worthless to them, for nothing they can buy brings them pleasure. Not everything in the cave is valuable: Pintel and Ragetti mistakenly bring a trunk of women's clothes.

PILE IT HIGH
Packed in chests, and heaped in untidy piles, gold and silver fill the cave. Precious jewels are strewn across the ground.

Pearl string once hung round the neck of a princess of Bavaria

Amethyst centrepiece of brooch is big as a pigeon's egg

PEARLS AND JEWELS
The treasure on *Isla de Muerta* includes huge quantities of gold and silver bars and coins. They came from raids on Spanish ships heading back to Seville from the country's colonies in Mexico and Peru. But some of the most valuable pieces are jewellery stolen from wealthy passengers on ships the *Black Pearl* attacked.

Lifting the Curse

Barbossa's crew brings Elizabeth to the island to return the last coin that she wears round her neck. They also aim to cut her with a flint knife. They think she's the daughter of 'Bootstrap Bill', and her blood will lift the curse – but they are wrong. She lied about who she is, giving them Will's surname.

Rowing to the Rescue

Jack and Will follow the crew of the *Black Pearl* to the island. From their hiding place, they helplessly watch as Barbossa prepares to sacrifice Elizabeth. When Jack won't stop the ceremony, Will suspects that Jack doesn't care what happens to her. He knocks Jack unconscious with an oar, and plucks Elizabeth to safety.

STABBED IN THE BACK

A skeleton with a sword in its back gives Will the idea that Jack is about to betray him.

We Have an Accord!

Captain Sparrow may be devious, but he's not a traitor – despite what Will believes. When Barbossa returns to *Isla de Muerta* to spill Will's blood, Jack proposes a partnership. "Wait to lift the curse until the opportune moment," he tells Barbossa. His canny deal saves Will's life.

Wedding Bells

White lace, flowers, a flowing dress and an altar. Everything is in place to make Elizabeth's wedding day perfect, except for one detail – the groom. Dark clouds fill the sky, and tears fill the bride's eyes. Surely Will would not let her down? Finally, as tropical rain soaks her bridal gown, Elizabeth learns the truth. Port Royal has a new boss. Her husband-to-be is in chains, accused of helping a pirate to escape and Elizabeth is charged with the same crime.

Beautiful golden gown ruined by rain

Unexpected Arrival

The cause of Elizabeth's misery is Lord Cutler Beckett, of the East India Trading Company. Clever and devious, he has become more powerful even than Governor Swann. Using his emergency powers "to rid the seas of piracy", he takes control of Port Royal.

Shackled!

Arrested as he dresses for his wedding, Will Turner arrives at the chapel in chains. Beckett reads out the charges against him: "...conspiring to set free a man lawfully convicted of crimes against the Empire, and condemned to death. For which the penalty is... death."

The heavy raindrops knock the petals from her bouquet, and the smile from her face

Wet Wedding

As if being stood up at the altar isn't enough, a rainstorm wrecks Elizabeth's wedding plans. Palm trees bend as the gale-force winds scatter chairs, and the guests run for cover. Elizabeth can't believe that Will would not turn up, and she sinks to her knees on the sodden grass.

Uninvited Guests
Lord Cutler Beckett's men take no chances. They surround the chapel where Elizabeth slumps in her soaking bridal gown. "My apologies for arriving without an invitation..." Beckett tells Governor Swann, with mock respect.

BAFFLED BRIDE
Hoisted to her feet by soldiers, Elizabeth cannot quite understand what's going on. When she turns to see Will in chains she realises that he has been arrested – and her dream of marrying the man she loves lies in tatters.

SILK SHOES
Elizabeth's wedding shoes are made from fine Chinese silk, with details picked out in tiny fresh-water pearls. They match her dress and train perfectly, but Wellington boots would have been better suited to her wedding-day weather.

Under Arrest!

Beckett's arrival with Will shocks Governor Swann. "By what authority have you arrested this man?" he demands. "By the Crown's authority," Beckett replies, and he has a pile of documents to prove it. Sure enough, Will's name is on a warrant, and he cannot deny that he is guilty. There's another warrant for Elizabeth, and one for Norrington, too.

In Search of Jack

When Will sets off in search of Jack Sparrow, he holds out no great hope of finding him. After all, Jack could be anywhere, and even the Royal Navy wasn't able to catch him. Will searches all over the Caribbean. The clues he finds lead him to a remote island... and terrible danger.

WHERE THERE'S A WILL THERE'S A WAY
When Will visits his jailed bride, he tells her Beckett has offered a deal: Elizabeth will go free if Will tracks down Jack. Will has no choice but to accept – though neither of them trust Beckett to keep his word.

Lord Beckett

As an executive of the East India Trading Company, Lord Cutler Beckett is a man with a mission. He aims to stamp out piracy wherever he finds it on the high seas. He has come to Port Royal to capture and execute scoundrels such as Jack Sparrow and the crew of the *Black Pearl*. He will do whatever he thinks is necessary to achieve his goal.

Beckett Beckons!

Although he pretends that he is interested only in stamping out piracy, Beckett has one more reason to capture Jack Sparrow. He knows all about the Dead Man's Chest, and about the heart of Davy Jones that beats inside it. Beckett believes that Jack Sparrow will lead him to the chest. Then he can control Davy Jones and eliminate pirates from the Seven Seas.

Mercer

Beckett arrives in Port Royal accompanied by his faithful assistant, Mercer. On the face of it Mercer is a clerk like any other – efficient, obedient and loyal, but he has a more sinister side. When doing his master's dirty work he is cruel and menacing and uses underhanded tactics, stopping at nothing to aid Beckett's pursuit of power.

STORMY ARRIVAL
Beckett uses his arrival in Port Royal to show how powerful he is. Royal Navy ships seal off the harbour. Marines march in step along the quay. Beckett himself is rowed ashore astride a white horse. He times his arrival so that he will interrupt Will and Elizabeth's wedding. He knows he can use them as bait to snare Jack.

Swann Defeated

Caught helping his daughter to flee the island, Governor Swann is imprisoned. Swann assumes that Beckett wants to govern Port Royal himself. But Beckett is more clever than Swann had realised. He wants Swann to stay on as governor but wants him to send good reports to the King in exchange for Elizabeth's safety.

Branded

Beckett brands pirates with a 'P.' This branding iron glows red hot once heated in a fire and allows him to inflict his special kind of punishment. He presses the searing letter onto the forearm of pirates he captures, leaving them permanently scarred.

The tip of the cane was used to brand Jack Sparrow

Pirate's Licence

Beckett knows that Jack will not want to hand over his compass so in exchange he offers him Letters of Marque. Signed by the King of England, these documents would make Jack a licensed pirate. His earlier crimes would be forgiven and he could legally attack the ships of any nation at war with England.

Royal seal and signature of King George

Leather wallet protects documents

Beckett has yet to fill in Jack's name on the letters

Beckett's seal and signature

Pocket Pistol

Beckett has made many enemies during his rise to power. Some would cheerfully kill him. To protect himself Beckett carries a pistol. Its short barrel allows him to slip it easily into a specially-made pocket in the lining of his frock coat.

Safety device stops gun going off by mistake

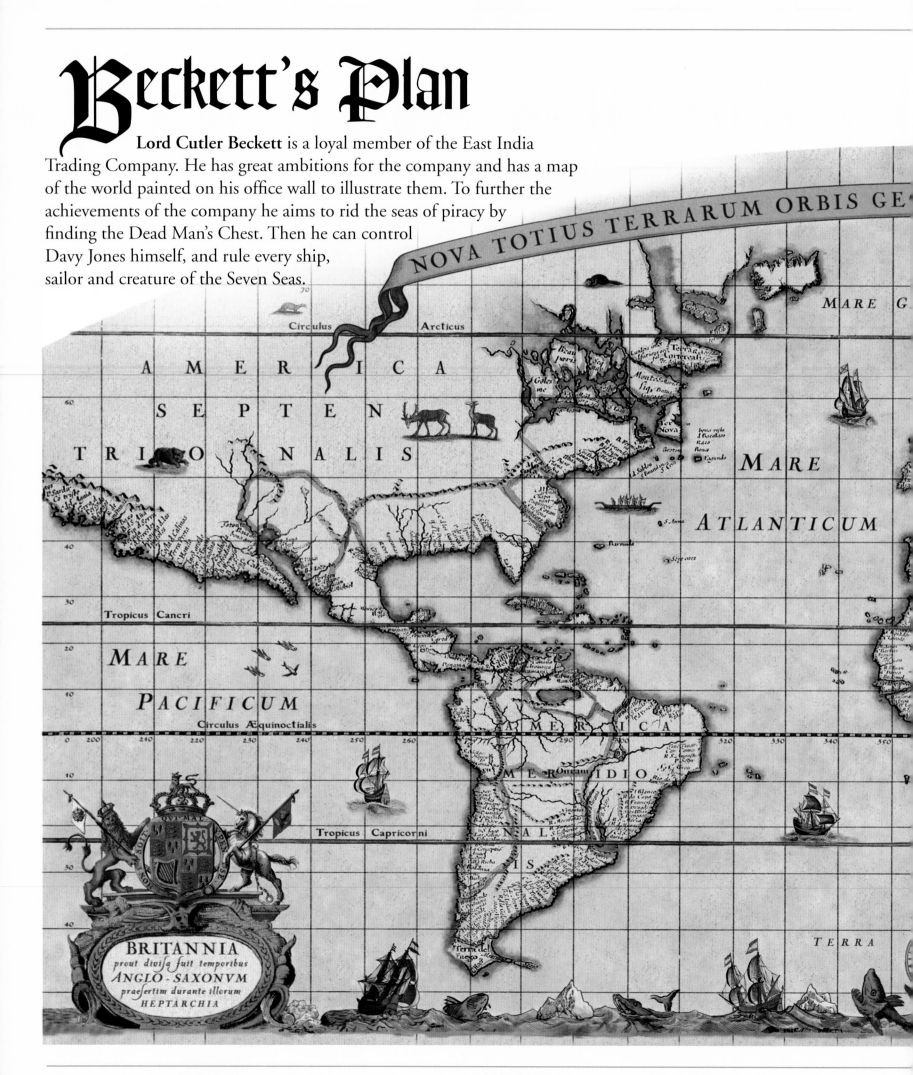

Beckett's Plan

Lord Cutler Beckett is a loyal member of the East India Trading Company. He has great ambitions for the company and has a map of the world painted on his office wall to illustrate them. To further the achievements of the company he aims to rid the seas of piracy by finding the Dead Man's Chest. Then he can control Davy Jones himself, and rule every ship, sailor and creature of the Seven Seas.

NOVA TOTIUS TERRARUM ORBIS GE

Circulus   Arcticus

MARE G.

A   M   E   R   I   C   A

S   E   P   T   E   N

MARE

T   R   I   O   N   A   L   I   S

Tropicus Cancri

MARE

ATLANTICUM

MERIDIO

M E R

PACIFICUM

A   M   E   R   I   C   A

Circulus Æquinoctialis

Tropicus Capricorni

N A L I

I   S

BRITANNIA
prout divisa fuit temporibus
ANGLO - SAXONVM
praesertim durante illorum
HEPTARCHIA

TERRA

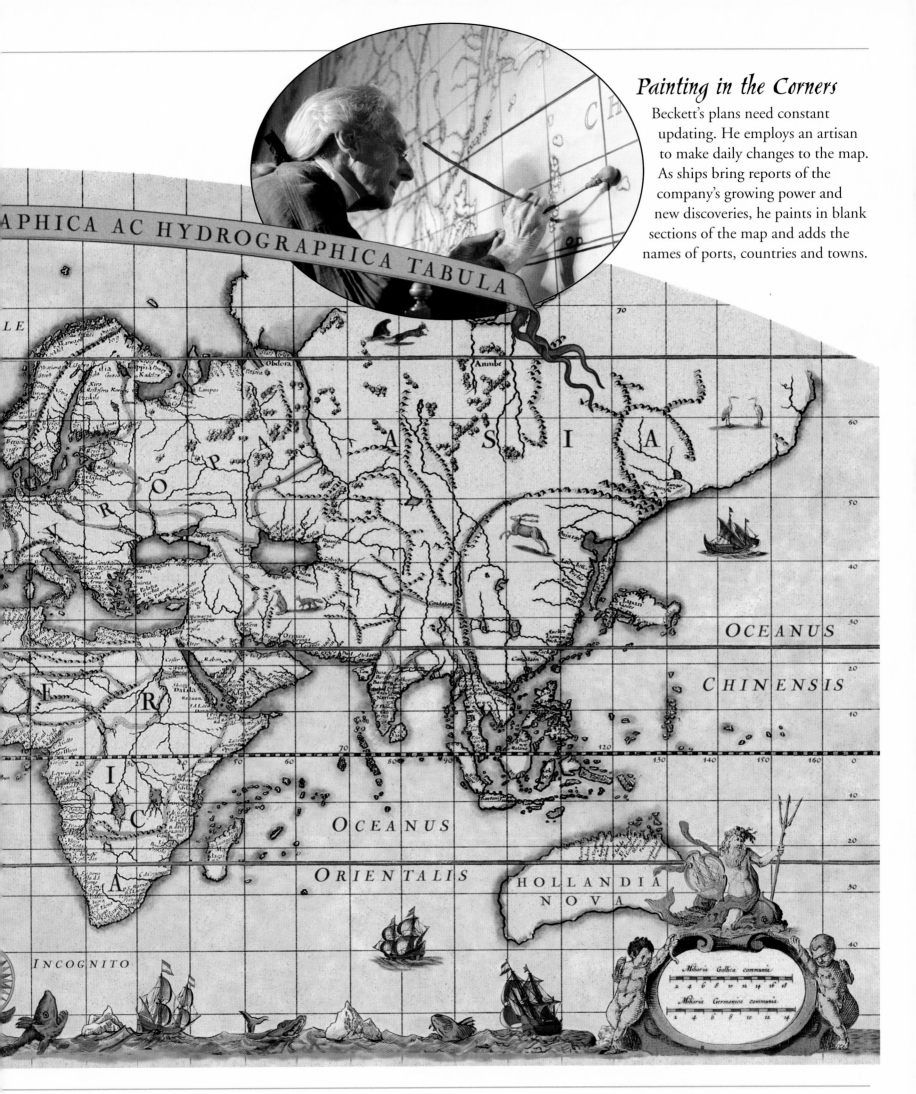

APHICA AC HYDROGRAPHICA TABULA

Painting in the Corners

Beckett's plans need constant updating. He employs an artisan to make daily changes to the map. As ships bring reports of the company's growing power and new discoveries, he paints in blank sections of the map and adds the names of ports, countries and towns.

EUROPA

ASIA

AFRICA

OCEANUS CHINENSIS

OCEANUS

ORIENTALIS

HOLLANDIA NOVA

INCOGNITO

Miliaria Gallica communia

Miliaria Germanica communia

East India Trading Co.

When European explorers first sailed to the East Indies, they were hypnotised by the fabulous wealth they found. The gold, silver, ivory, silk and exotic spices lured traders hungry for a profit. English merchants were particularly successful in sponsoring trading voyages. The East India Trading Company, the company they set up, grew in size and power and controlled much of India's trade. Eager to expand still further, the powerful men at the head of the company now looked to the rich plantations of the Caribbean.

Coat of Arms

The company's gold and maroon coat of arms shows how grand its aims are. Beneath waving pennants, sea lions support a shield dotted with ships and roses. The Latin slogan on a ribbon underneath means 'Nothing can harm us when God leads us'.

Lord Cutler Beckett

Ambitious and ruthless, Cutler Beckett is in the Caribbean to oversee the expansion. He would be delighted to change the company's name to the East and West India Trading Company. But he knows that he can make no progress until he has stamped out the scourge of piracy.

Derricks lower heavy cargo into the hold

Loading Up

Tied up at Port Royal docks, an East India Trading Company ship loads up. Sugar – as sugar loaves or molasses – fills most of her hold, and barrels of rum much of the remainder. But there's still room for a bewildering variety of other goods to trade between the islands.

Company uses much smaller ships in the Caribbean than the huge East Indiamen that sail to India

Boxes, Bundles and Bales

Once the ship's officers have completed the company's business at the ports they visit, they are allowed to do a little trading on their own account. (They do a little smuggling, too, even though it's strictly forbidden.) Along the quayside the merchants and farmers of Port Royal line up to load the officer's purchases.

Send in the Marines!

The East India Trading Company has grown so large that a threat to the company is a threat to Britain itself. So the government takes care to protect the company, supplying marines to guard its ships and a Royal Navy escort when dangerous pirates such as Jack Sparrow are abroad.

COMPANY TRADEMARK

Stamped, stencilled and painted on every box, bundle and barrel loaded aboard the ship, is the trademark of the East India Trading Company. Separated by triple crosses, the company's initials act as a guarantee of quality – and also discourage petty thieves.

Wooden crate contains colourful silk from the Far East, a luxury prized in the Caribbean

Jack's Bargain

Pirates never buy their ships. Some 'borrow' them. Most steal them. A few trade them in crooked deals. The *Black Pearl*, however, is like no other ship, and Jack Sparrow is no ordinary pirate. What brought them together was a dark and dangerous bargain. Thirteen years ago Jack made a deal with Davy Jones. The commander of the oceans raised the *Black Pearl* from the depths in exchange for Jack's soul. Now the time has come for Jack to keep his side of the bargain.

Seashells and barnacles grow from his face

Davy Jones' Messenger

In a strange twist of fate it is Will's father, 'Bootstrap Bill' who brings Jack the bad news. After Bootstrap was sent overboard by Barbossa, Davy Jones offered to save him if he pledged to serve on the *Flying Dutchman* for a century. Ever since Bill has been a helpless crewman for the ocean's ruler.

NIGHTMARE
At first Jack thinks he's had too much rum. He goes to look for another bottle, and finds it encrusted with barnacles. Inside it there's only sand. When Bootstrap appears from the shadows Jack is surpised. "Is this a dream?" he asks, hoping he'll wake up soon.

TIME TO SETTLE A DEBT
Bootstrap reminds Jack of his bargain with Davy Jones saying "the terms what applied to me applied to you, too: one soul, bound to crew upon his ship for a lifetime". Either Jack must give himself up or Jones' sea beast will deliver him to its master.

*Barnacles cling to the
handle and guard*

BOOTSTRAP'S SWORD

Though it's forged from the native
iron of the sea bed, Bootstrap's sword does not
look like much. A thick coating of rust has dulled and blunted
the once-gleaming blade. However, in Bill's hands it's a lethal
weapon. He swings it with truly terrifying power, cutting
through heavy ships' timbers as if they were seaweed.

The Black Spot

Jack is a marked man after his visit from
'Bootstrap Bill'. Staring at his hand in horror, he
sees the Black Spot appear in the middle of his
palm. It's a sign that Davy Jones' obedient sea
beast will find him wherever he flees on the
Seven Seas. The merciless Kraken will drag Jack
down to Davy Jones' Locker to repay his debt.

Cannibal Island

In the most remote corner of the Caribbean sea lies a mysterious island. It is missing from ocean charts and far from all normal shipping routes. Its warlike people, the Pelegostos, have a grim secret: they relish the taste of 'long pork' – human flesh. It is to this very island that the unfortunate Jack Sparrow flees when he is cursed with the BLACK SPOT!

Rickety bridges made from jungle vines allow the cannibals to cross the gaping ravines that carve up the island.

CANNIBAL CLAN

Painted, pierced, masked and, above all, hungry, the cannibals make a fearsome sight. Their carefully-applied face and body paint isn't just decorative. It makes them blend in perfectly with the dripping tropical rainforest that covers their island home. For weapons they use spears, machetes and blow-pipes with drugged darts.

HOME SWEET HOME

Woven from plant fibres, the cannibal huts look like the homes of funnel-web spiders. Despite their fragile appearance, they provide shelter from heavy tropical storms.

DANCE OF DEATH

Half ballet, half funeral march, this tribal dance celebrates a hearty meal. They dance with a special frenzy: Jack Sparrow is on the menu, and by eating him (they believe) they will release the god from his human prison.

WASTE NOT WANT NOT

This bone pile is not just leftovers. The tops of skulls make useful drinking cups and eye sockets neatly hold candles upright.

The village is built on the flat top of one of the island's soaring peaks.

The Pelegostos Tribe

Will follows Jack to a remote and apparently deserted island. He senses he is in terrible danger when the pilot of the shrimp boat that ferries him there is a little too keen to get away. As Will steps onto the beach there is an eerie silence, broken only when Cotton's parrot lands on a tree squawking "Don't eat me!". As Will hacks his way inland contemplating the parrots peculiar words, little does he realise he's walking straight into a trap.

Rainforest Raiders

Will does not see the crouching figures that lie in wait for him. The patterns of their body painting form a perfect camouflage against the background of leaves and creepers. He is captured before he even realises he's being watched.

RELUCTANT LEADER

The Pelegostos tribe has adopted Jack as its king! He is given a grim necklace made from toes and his face is painted with four pairs of scary staring eyes.

ON THE THRONE

Jack sits on a grand throne decorated with skulls and bones at the heart of the cannibal village. He has picked up the local language and talks to his subjects in grunts, clicks and teeth-grinding sounds.

54

Will on a Stick

Once they have captured Will, the hunters truss him up like an animal, and carry him to their village. There Will is delighted to see Jack, and assumes he will soon be free. But when Jack pretends not to recognise him and whispers, "Save me!" Will realises that he and Jack face the same gruesome fate.

Badges of Royalty

As cannibal king, Jack gets to wear a special necklace of human toes. His feather sceptre commands all who see it to obey him (as long as he doesn't ask for freedom).

Sinews hold the feathers in place

Grisly toe garland

The Crew Escapes

Though they are trapped inside a cage made out of human bones, Will and the crew of the *Black Pearl* manage to escape, taking their prison with them. They make a dash for the beach, the ship and freedom!

Sparrow Kebab

Before the cannibals can barbecue him, Jack escapes too. The wooden stake tied to his back makes a handy vaulting pole, springing him across a jungle ravine.

Sprint for the Ship

Just as the *Black Pearl* sets sail, Captain Jack Sparrow dashes down the beach, and jumps on board. The cannibals will need to find a new dinner 'guest'.

The Bayou

Jack Sparrow realises he will need help to track down Davy Jones. So he goes looking for someone he knows he can rely on, voodoo priestess Tia Dalma. The journey to the tumbledown shack where she lives is not an easy one. Jack, Will and the crew have to find their way through the spooky cypress forest. They launch two longboats from the *Black Pearl*, and cautiously paddle up the Pantano River. As they venture further into the forest a sense of unease descends upon them as the tall trees block out the sunlight, alligators stir on mud banks and the curious swamp people watch them silently from the river banks.

Tree House

Tia Dalma's shack clings to the branches of a tree in a distant part of the swamp. Though it glows brightly, the hut seems to suck the light out of the surrounding forest. Every kind of timber makes up the walls and roof. In between the forest logs are nailed planks from coffins, and parts of discarded canoes patch the roof.

"HAVE A GOOD TRIP!"

Jack doesn't like the journey through the forest at all. Though he seems to know where he is going, he keeps a tight grip on the rope, and glances about himself nervously all the time. His travelling companions are just as frightened. They are worried about Jack, too. "What is it that has Jack spooked?" asks Will. "Nothing can keep Jack Sparrow from the sea".

FOREST BEASTS

The crew stare wide-eyed at the strangely coloured reptiles that scuttle nimbly along the branches of the trees.

SILENT AUDIENCE

Though the people of the swamp do them no harm, Jack and the others get nervous just from being watched so closely. A pair of eyes seems to peer at them from every shadow. They are not so worried by the figures they can see clearly, like this old man sitting in a rocking chair on his porch, with a dog at his feet. It's what they can't see clearly that they fear most, such as the figures half hidden in the leaves.

UP THE LADDER

At Tia Dalma's shack, a ladder leads up from the water, and Jack climbs it. "Tia Dalma and I go way back," he brags. "Thick as thieves. Nigh inseparable, we were. I'll handle this." Though he puts on a brave face, he's not sure of himself, and whispers "guard my back" to Gibbs.

SPOOKY PROCESSION

When the meeting is over, Jack's crew follow him down the ladder, and clamber gratefully into the canoes. They have an uncanny feeling that this won't be their last visit to the cypress forest. Though each of them silently swears that they will never return to this creepy place, they all know that they can't cheat destiny.

Tia Dalma's Shack

Perched in a tree top near the mouth of the Pantano River is a shack belonging to voodoo priestess, Tia Dalma. It is a damp and gloomy world where nothing is quite what it seems to be. But, judging Tia Dalma by her humble home is a mistake. She has uncanny powers to foretell the future, to summon up demons and to look deep into men's souls. So it's to this mysterious and beautiful priestess that Jack turns when he wants to find Davy Jones.

Claw Reading

Tia Dalma has amazing abilities and uses them to help her old 'friend' Jack. With a clatter of crab claws on a rough wooden table, the priestess can see what ordinary mortals cannot. She gently throws the claws on the table and 'reads' their positions to discern the whereabouts of Davy Jones and his crew.

Delicate pattern accentuates her hypnotic eyes

MAGIC NECKLACE

From a silver chain round Tia Dalma's neck hangs a curious pendant. Though the crab-shaped pendant is tarnished and has dulled with age, a mysterious face is still visible.

Chain made from the purest of silver

Crab claws

Dried plants are ground down to make potions

Jar holds locks of sirens' hair

Preserved sea snake

Swamp toad spawn used to heal many ailments

Vials filled with spider venom

On Land – Even at Sea

Tia Dalma tells Jack what he wants to know: where to find the *Flying Dutchman* and its captain, Davy Jones. To protect him from Davy's power, she gives Jack a jar of dirt, so that he'll always be near land – and safety.

A SIGHT FOR SORE EYES

Tia's shack is teeming with jars of weird objects and one in particular has Ragetti transfixed. In an iron-bound jar hanging from a rafter, float dozens of staring eyeballs. For most this grisly sight would be sickening but for Ragetti the eyeballs are beautiful to behold. For as long as he can remember he has longed to exchange his wooden eye for the real thing and maybe now his dream will come true.

STRANGE ATTRACTION

Will's boyish good looks charm Tia Dalma. As soon as he enters the shack, she beams an inviting smile at him. Jack flatters himself that the grin is for him, and is shocked when his old sweetheart ignores him. She touches Will's face with her hand. "You have a touch of destiny in you, William Turner..." she tells him: though they have never met before, she knows his name.

Souls for Sale

In a terrifying bargain with Davy Jones, Jack Sparrow has just three days to find 100 human souls. If he succeeds, he will be a free man once more. If he fails, he faces a life of slavery, serving Jones on the *Flying Dutchman*. Fortunately, Jack knows just the place to look for souls – the *Faithful Bride* tavern on the island of Tortuga. With help from Gibbs, Jack reckons he can easily find enough desperate men to fulfil his side of the bargain. He might even do it before time runs out.

Queuing to Sell their Souls

The misfits who line up in the tavern have no idea of the fate Jack has in mind for them. Each man is blighted with an ailment – some are old and practically blind, a few are lame and many have never set foot upon a ship in their lives. "What makes you think you're worthy to crew on the *Black Pearl*?" Gibbs asks them one by one. Their answers are pathetic, but Gibbs does not care. Anyone will do – as long as they have a soul to sell, and can sign on the dotted line.

Table in the tavern becomes Gibbs' desk

Pile of recruiting papers

Surprise Recruit

When James Norrington joins the queue, Gibbs does not recognise him at first. Disgraced and no longer a commodore, he claims that he is determined to go back to sea and is even willing to join the pirates he once hunted. But old habits die hard and Norrington pulls out a gun and takes aim at Jack.

SHARING A STY
Norrington's foolishness with the gun causes chaos. Drunken pirates love to fight, and here at last is the perfect excuse for a brawl. Norrington is on the losing side, and ends up in the gutter with the pigs.

NORRINGTON AND MERCER
Elizabeth leaves Norrington alone at the quayside where he is approached by Beckett's clerk, Mercer. In the shadows Mercer strikes a deal with the disgraced former commodore on behalf of his master.

THE BROKEN COMPASS
Just as the *Black Pearl* is about to sail, Jack gets another surprise recruit. It's Elizabeth, cunningly disguised as a sailor boy. Jack lies about how he betrayed Will – then realises that Elizabeth's desire to rescue her fiancé will lead him to the chest. He tells her that the only way to save Will is to find the Dead Man's Chest that contains the heart of Davy Jones, knowing that her greatest wish will be to locate the chest. He hands her his compass and as he predicted the needle swings and holds steady in one direction, giving them their heading.

Davy Jones

Peaks of hat resemble devil horns

Tentacles

Imagine a creature half human, half sea beast, with black eyes as soulless as a shark's, a claw for an arm and a beard made of octopus tentacles. This nightmarish creature is Davy Jones, legendary ruler of the ocean depths. Doomed to cruise the oceans forever in his ghost-ship the *Flying Dutchman*, Jones offers drowning mariners the chance to live by joining his crew – a fate that turns out to be worse than death.

Heartless Beast

According to legend, Davy Jones fell in love with a woman "as harsh and untameable as the sea". He never stopped loving her and the pain it caused him was too much for him to bear so he carved out his heart and locked it away in a chest. He keeps the key to the chest with him at all times and the location of the chest is a closely guarded secret.

'BOOTSTRAP BILL'
Will Turner's father, 'Bootstrap Bill', traded his soul with Davy Jones. A relatively new member of the *Flying Dutchman*'s crew, he remains more human than sea creature.

Stem is made from silver mined below the sea bed

Crab claw

PIPING HOT
Carved from whalebone, Davy's pipe is rarely out of his mouth. He fills it with a mysterious mixture that burns so fiercely that it stays alight even in the deepest ocean.

Poor Wyvern!

The longer that
the mariners sail on the
Flying Dutchman, the worse
is their fate, for they slowly
become part of the ship. Wyvern
is almost as wooden as the ship's
beams and knuckles. There's still a bit
of human left in him, though, and he helps
Will find the key to the Dead Man's Chest.

*Wyvern's outstretched arm
grips a ship's lantern*

Father and Son

Reunited with his son on the
deck of the *Flying Dutchman*,
'Bootstrap Bill' only recognises
Will as he's about to get a
lashing. He is determined to
help his son to escape from
Jones' clutches.

*The key to the
chest has a unique
double-stem
design*

THE KEY TO JONES' HEART

Will shows Bootstrap the outline of the
key that Jack obtained in the Turkish prison.
Then, in a dangerous game of Liar's Dice, they
learn that Jones keeps it on a lanyard round his neck.
While Bootstrap stands watch, his son sneaks in to Jones'
cabin, and snatches the key from the sleeping captain.

*Decorated
with carvings
of sea snakes*

*Wyvern is covered in co[...]
and barnacles and is
almost indistinguishabl[...]
from the ship's hull*

DEAD MAN'S CHEST

Davy Jones' heart still
beats inside the Dead Man's
Chest. Will learns that if can
find the chest, open it and stab
the beating heart, Davy Jones
will die. The doomed crewmen
of the *Flying Dutchman* will
at last be released from
their fiendish bargain.

*Elaborate lock
resembles both a
heart and a crab*

e Flying Dutchman

...en mariners awake screaming, it's because they
...hostly ship and its terrifying barnacled crew.
...e *Flying Dutchman* rises from the ocean depths, its
...aweed and its sails glowing like fire. It speeds across
...all other ships are becalmed. Its very timbers sigh
... weighed down with a century of weary toil. When
...d and are doomed to drown they soon realise that
...t just a myth; the ship appears before their eyes and
...ked from the jaws of death and given the option to
...st of Davy Jones' ship.

...sic

...g music envelops
... Davy Jones'
...pears to have
...he deck.
...keyboard for
...g all his
...ful melodies.
... a carving of a
...ing hair and
...tures. As he
...rmented by
...nsfixed by the
... look at her.

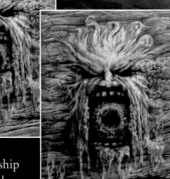

...ANNON'S MOUTH
...t of the *Dutchman*
...be alive. Even the
...grimace with human faces. When the ship
...he attack, the row of mouths that line the
...wide to show the bronze cannons within

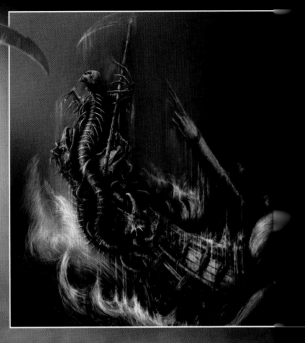

GRIM FIGUREHEAD

At the bows of the ghost-ship hangs a carved statue of the Grim Reaper. This legendary figure cuts off lives as if cutting corn with his scythe. It's a fitting figurehead. For Jones no longer simply collects the souls of drowning sailors. Now he drags them to their doom.

CAPTAIN'S CABIN

At the heart of the ship, Jones' cabin shimmers with the light of a million glowing deep-sea creatures. Its ornate panels are carved from the wrecks of sunken ships.

LAMPS ASTERN

Few human sailors ever see the stern of the *Flying Dutchman* – or if they do, it's the last thing they see. The pattern of windows in the ship's great cabin glow like the teeth of a grinning mouth. The deck above is decorated with the intertwined skeletons of ferocious sea beasts.

Davy Jones' Crew

A Frightful Sight
Although Davy Jones' crew has an assortment of deadly weapons, they are seldom needed. Just the sight of them is enough to scare anyone to death!

Eye

Razor-sharp teeth

Grey, thick skin resembles that of a shark

Maccus' boarding axe comes in handy for severing ropes and limbs.

The sound of their sodden, barnacle encrusted feet landing upon your deck in the dead of night is enough to make most sailors hurl themselves into the sea in panic. These marine marauders are the desperate souls who have chosen one hundred years with Davy Jones in preference to facing death's final judgement.

Koleniko
This prickly pirate faces the grotesque fate of gradually swelling into the form of a human blowfish. His bloated eye misses little when reading the night stars and he is often called upon for his navigational skills. He can be easily drawn into a game of Liar's Dice with Maccus and Clanker.

Crab-like legs sprout from arm

Sharp spines

Fish eye

Maccus
Instantly recognised by his hammerhead, the *Flying Dutchman*'s first mate relishes any dirty work doled out to him. With a stricken vessel in his sights, Maccus is the first into action, using those extra eyes to count the dead and round up potential new recruits for his captain.

Legs covered in barnacles

Lobster claws
grow out of head

Seahorse
eyes

Algae-covered
hat

Seaweed hair

Mussels

Sea
anemones

The Twins

Two heads are better than one, especially
when it comes to terrifying your foes. These
inseparable brothers are not only becoming
part of the ship, they are becoming part
of each other. This dire double act
slave away at the thankless
mechanical tasks
that keep their
vessel going.

Tiny parasitic
crustaceans cement the
twins' toes together into
calcified blocks.

Clanker

Down on your
marrow bones and
pray! This barnacle-
browed blackguard wields
chainshot with devastating
effect. His wicked laugh can
be heard echoing around the ship,
especially when he sees
others suffer.

Shipmates

Coral-covered, weed-wrapped, polyp-pimpled grotesques, these terrifying creatures are more loyal members of Davy Jones' ruthless gang. While they are under the curse of the *Flying Dutchman*, they cannot be killed, and therefore, they know no fear. No murderous mission they undertake can be any more nightmarish and punishing than daily life on their own ship. Many regret choosing to serve their harsh captain, for as he points out – life is cruel, why should the afterlife be any different?

Mouth similar to that of a piranha

The boatswain prefers a cutlass with a large cup-shaped handguard.

Body covered in thick layer of slimy seaweed

JIMMY LEGS

Davy Jones' bosun is a hard taskmaster who enjoys demanding the impossible as he orders the crew to work. Punishments are his speciality, and he prides himself on cleaving flesh from bone with every swing of his cat-of-nine-tails.

GREENBEARD

Almost completely smothered in seaweed, Greenbeard has more in common with vegetable-matter now than humanity, and as such no longer needs to rest or eat. Merciless and oblivious of his own flesh-and blood past, he feels no pity for the sailors he hurls into the deep if they refuse his captain's kind offer to join up.

Over time boot has become part of leg

The jagged snout of a saw-fish makes an effective weapon

Shark teeth tied to pieces of wood form a lethal knuckle duster

Head is crested with fire coral

Anemone eyes

Sharp, curved teeth

Starfish hand

Eel protrudes from stomach

QUITTANCE
With anatomy similar to that of a starfish, over time Quittance is able to regenerate limbs that are damaged or lost during battles.

Stinging tentacles

Human bone fuses with dead coral structures to form tough exterior skeleton

Palafico attacks with a combination of rusty rapier and crusty cutlass.

PALAFICO
With stinging tentacles sprouting from his anemone eyes, Palafico may appear more reef than man, but he retains his human values and deems it appropriate that Captain Jack goes down with his ship at the attack of the Kraken. He fights with a sword in each hand and is hard to disarm as his blades are becoming part of his body. He enjoys snacking on live fish.

Seaweed hangs from sword

Isla Cruces

In the hands of Elizabeth, Jack's compass leads them to *Isla Cruces*. As the *Black Pearl* approaches the deserted island, Jack senses that he is just moments away from finding the Dead Man's Chest and being free of the terrible debt he owes Davy Jones. But unbeknown to Jack there are others who have set their sights on the chest...

Buried Treasure

Elizabeth leads them to the spot where the chest lies and they start to dig. Suddenly, a spade makes a hollow thud and Jack brushes away the sand to reveal a large chest. He pulls it out and hastily breaks the lock with the shovel.

Missing a Beat
From the chest Jack pulls out mementoes of Jones' past love. Finally they hear the heart beating within a smaller chest.

Beach Front Battle
At last Jack has what he wants and can use the heart to make Jones call off the Kraken, but Will appears with the key and wants to stab the heart to release his father from slavery on board the *Flying Dutchman*. When Norrington also stakes his claim on the heart in order to regain his honour, a battle for the key ensues.

Nautical Nasties

Jack, Norrington and Will are busy fighting, unaware that the *Flying Dutchman* is looming ominously just offshore. Davy Jones cannot set foot upon land so he sends his ferocious crewmen to retrieve his heart. They emerge menacingly from the crystal-clear waters and make their way up the shore.

A Terrible Temptation

Having seen the *Dutchman* appear, Pintel and Ragetti flee for their lives only to find the others fighting. Realising that everyone else is distracted they can't resist the opportunity to steal the precious chest, and make their escape into the dense jungle carrying it between them.

MAKING AN ESCAPE

Pintel and Ragetti's good fortune is short-lived and they soon regret taking the chest. Nothing could prepare them for their encounter with Jones' barnacle-encrusted army.

BALANCING ACT

When Jack, Will and Norrington find themselves in an old mill, their battle takes on an unexpected twist. Will and Norrington end up balancing upon a huge mill wheel which breaks loose and hurtles through the jungle.

Journey's End

After a tireless fight with Will, Jack and the crew of the *Flying Dutchman*, Norrington arrives filthy and bedraggled in Beckett's office. After a battle with so many twists and turns, who eventually won the heart? If Norrington can produce it he'll redeem himself and regain his place in society. But perhaps the heart is with Jack on the *Black Pearl* or even back with its owner, Davy Jones...

The Kraken

The Kraken is Davy Jones' obedient leviathan, sent to prey on unwary ships and mariners. With a hideous roar and a towering wave of foam and spray, a gigantic tentacle breaks the surface of the sea. Cold, clammy, slimy and immensely strong, it wraps itself around the deck of a boat and crushes it like matchwood. Then the head of the sea monster slowly rises from the waves. On its breath the terrified ship's crew smell the rotting corpses of a thousand drowned sailors. Its rolling eyes briefly focus, then it dives, dragging the doomed ship down to Davy Jones' Locker. The Kraken has struck again!

Sailors struggle to hold on to the remains of their ship

The Kraken wraps its tentacles around the ship before it pulls it down into the sea.

What Lies Beneath

The Kraken appears without warning, rising suddenly from the depths and giving sailors no chance to flee. Incredibly, this gigantic creature is able to sneak up on a ship unnoticed. It uses its powerful suckers to pull itself silently along the rocks on the ocean floor, far below the sight of sailors. Then, when it is directly under its prey – it attacks!

No ship stands a chance against the mighty Kraken. The Edinburgh *is crushed like matchwood.*

The huge suckers on the Kraken's tentacles are strong enough to pull the flesh clean away from a sailor's face.

The beast uses the tips of its tentacles to feel its way around a ship before deciding where to strike next.

Powerful tentacles slam into the deck, breaking it in two

Even in calm waters the Kraken causes the sea to churn and swirl as it rises from the depths.

SEA MONSTER

For centuries this beast of the deep has inspired fear amongst sailors. Few have seen the Kraken and lived to tell the tale. The monster is said to be the length of 10 ships, with immensely strong tentacles and a huge gaping mouth filled with rows of razor-sharp teeth.

Singapore

It may look like a dilapidated, stinking shanty town, but this murky harbour conceals priceless secrets that can lead pirates to treasures beyond their dreams. Elizabeth and Barbossa make their way here in search of a little help in their quest to rescue Captain Jack Sparrow. All they want is a spare ship and a crew prepared to voyage to World's End – and they're hoping to catch ruthless Pirate Lord Sao Feng in a good mood...

To blend in with the locals Elizabeth wears a broad-rimmed hat made from hand-woven bamboo.

Visitors Beware!

Unsavoury characters, miserable sea-scum and sneaky cut-purses lurk amidst the glow of the traditional red paper lanterns strung across the crooked bridges of the harbour.

HIDDEN EYES

Chart-makers, glass-blowers or wizened old fishermen – countless inscrutable characters haunt the narrow byways of the port. They may appear to be going about their own business, but many are part of Sao Feng's network of spies and whisperers, passing on word of any new arrivals back to their master. Not many dodgy dealings go unnoticed in these quarters, as those who aren't in the pay of Sao Feng are generally spying for the East India Company.

Loose-fitting trousers made from hemp, a rough fabric woven from plant fibres

MARKET PLACE

Singapore's market is truly an assault on the senses. Stalls are crammed with sacks of herbs, spices, rice, noodles, beans and other goods. The air is filled with the pungent odour of fish heads, eels, cow tongues, frogs and a turtle or two, mingled with the sweet fragrance of exotic fruits and vegetables.

Wooden pole used
to steer the canoe

Stone foundations from
16th century fort

Mist rises from the
murky water
providing ideal cover
for nefarious deeds

Crabbing baskets can
be used to smuggle
contraband

Flat-bottomed
pea-pod canoe

The Bath House

Deep within the shadowy backwaters of this
busy port is a hallowed haunt which only the most
privileged – and the most notorious – are allowed to
visit. Elizabeth and Barbossa seek Sao Feng's hidden
headquarters and most sacred retreat – the bath house.

Assassin's steel-
ribbed fan

DEMURE BUT DEADLY

Sao Feng doesn't just surround himself with
beautiful women because he has a weakness
for a pretty face. He knows they make
deadly personal guards. The ornamental
fan seen here can also serve as a weapon,
with slashing, bladed ribs.

LADIES OF THE NIGHT

Don't be fooled by the jasmine
flowers and silken robes of the ladies
of the town – they make look pretty,
but they can soon turn ugly.

Sao Feng

Pirate Lord of Singapore and scourge of the South China Sea, Sao Feng is feared from Malaya to Macao. Shrewd and subtle-witted, he is not one to shirk from danger, as the many scars which score his shaven head reveal. This dignified double-dealer holds a dark secret in his heart. In return for a promise of safety from the East India Company, he would quite happily send his pirate brethren to the gallows.

Ancient duelling scars

HOLDING COURT
This Pirate Lord enjoys the trappings of glory and holds court like a true emperor, with candles, incense and concubines.

Shoulder guard decorated with bronze amulets

SIGN OF THE DRAGON
In the Orient, the dragon is a sign of power, imperial might and strength in war. Sao Feng bears this tattoo as do his loyal followers.

Red fabric wrapped around ring for luck

Jade insets on armour-plated belt

LUCKY RING
Sao Feng's preferred precious stone is jade because he believes it confers safety, long-life and good fortune. A large jade stone is set in his antique gold ring.

Jade

Traditional Chinese martial sword designed to be wielded with two-hands

Long heavy blade can shear off metal armour

Black lacquered wooden scabbard

Wrought iron scabbard throat

Skilled Combatant

Sao Feng gained notoriety for his ruthlessness in combat. His weapon of choice is a traditional Chinese sword but he also carries a pistol and is a skilled marksman. An innovative man, Sao Feng is just as lethal using everyday sailors' tools, like a wooden fid, against his enemies.

Woven straw labourer's hat

SOFT SPOT

Cold-hearted in his dealings with men, Sao Feng enjoys the challenge of winning over a proud and beautiful woman. When Elizabeth questions his courage and accuses him of cowering in his bath water while his ships rot in the harbour, he doesn't resent her words – they simply pique his interest in her special spirit.

Studded leather cloak

Faithful Follower

Tai Huang is the captain of Sao Feng's guards. Although proud to do any dirty work his boss can dream up, he sometimes regrets having the idea of using the sewer system as a secret underground highway.

IN GRAVE DANGER

Will's life is in peril when he is captured whilst trying to steal navigational charts from Sao Feng's uncle's temple.

JUNK YARD

Sao Feng's pride and joy, the *Empress*, could be heading for Davy Jones' junk yard, as it is doomed for a fatal encounter with a certain supernatural ship....

French single-shot flintlock pistol

The Bath House

The ultimate luxury in Sao Feng's damp and dismal domain – the steaming, damp-scented paradise of a private bath house. This temple to steamy indulgence is more than just a place to relax. Its mysterious mists create the perfect atmosphere for a piratical business meeting. And if the encounter does not go as planned, then the filthy waters are an ideal place to conceal weapons.

A hot rinse removes the blood and gunpowder

Fungus even grows on the bathers

The damp conditions of the bath house are perfect for the fungi which sprout from every surface.

Surprise Guest

Unbeknown to Elizabeth and Barbossa, a close friend of theirs has also been attending their meeting – Will Turner. And he has been attending it in the bottom of a tub of ice-water. Schooled in the art of surprise, Sao Feng dramatically reveals Will to his guests. If they don't talk quickly, then Will will not be present at the meeting for long – well, not in one piece, anyway.

The Boiler Room

It may look dilapidated and decrepit from the outside, but inside the bath house is served by a highly advanced and sophisticated array of pipes and boilers – not to mention the efforts of two men sweating away, as they heave at the giant bellows suspended over their heads.

Wood and leather bellows

Being short helps when operating the bellows as there is little room under the bath house.

THE SWEAT SHOP

Even on shore Sao Feng runs a tight ship and his bath house workers must ensure that there is a constant supply of hot water and steam. A complicated network of pipes made from bamboo, transport the hot steam from the boiler room to the bath tubs above.

Personal Dressers

One of the perks of being a Pirate Lord is not having to get yourself dressed. Lian and Park, Sao Feng's personal attendants, take care of that, and they are quite capable of taking care of any intruders too. Those steel chopsticks pinning up their hair also double as vicious weapons.

Chopsticks can be used as weapons

Attendant is beautiful but deadly

STEAM CLEANED

Sao Feng finds that the hot steam soothes away his tensions – especially useful when the tranquillity of his bath house disappears rapidly with Barbossa and Elizabeth's arrival.

Long fingernails are a symbol of wealth and a high status because they signify that Sao Feng does not do manual work.

A Cunning Plan

Pirates cut deals for many reasons: because pooling resources shows wisdom, or perhaps because compromise is a sign of maturity. But usually they make deals for one reason – to save their own scrawny necks. Barbossa and Elizabeth go to Sao Feng's bath house with one aim in mind – to obtain his ancient sea charts that will lead them to World's End and Jack Sparrow. They plan to strike an amicable deal with Sao Feng but just in case, their crew is on standby, waiting for the opportune moment.

TIA DALMA'S PUSH-CART
Pirates are known for their bizarre ingenuity. Tia Dalma's cart, selling canaries, potions and snacks, houses a keg of quality gunpowder, ready to go off on a very short fuse.

Though it means double-crossing almost everyone he knows, Will is willing to do so for the sake of his father 'Bootstrap Bill'.

Triple-crosser

Will Turner has his own agenda for the meeting with Sao Feng. He has double-crossed Barbossa, he's ready to cross Jack Sparrow – and now he's offering Sao Feng a deal. So why should the Pirate Lord of Singapore trust such a slippery customer? Because, Will explains, the others stand in the way of what he wants whereas Sao Feng can help him get it – his father's freedom from the *Flying Dutchman*.

Sao Feng promises to slit Will's throat if he betrays him.

Using Your Nut

No mission would be complete without some reinforcements ready to wade in when things start to go wrong. If anyone can achieve the impossible it's Pintel, Gibbs, Ragetti, Cotton and Marty – who actually specialise in making things look impossible in the first place. The unsinkable crew manage to slip through the ring of enemy agents, disguised as coconuts!

Hollow reed snorkel

Coconut shell

Creeper twine chinstrap

COCONUT CAMOUFLAGE

It's not unusual to see rubbish drifting in Singapore so no-one suspects anything when a couple of coconuts float gently on the water. But these are no ordinary coconuts – they have been converted into underwater breathing devices with added camouflage – in other words, coconut skull-caps with reed breathing pipes.

IN HOT WATER

Once under the Bath House the pirates plant grenades in the floor joists to blast an escape route for their bosses. Well, if ever there was an ideal place for a clean getaway....

Tell-tale Sign

When it emerges that Sao Feng has captured Will, Barbossa and Elizabeth try to pretend that they have never seen him before but when Sao Feng prepares to make a fid-shaped hole in her fiancé, Elizabeth can't help but betray her real feelings.

Elizabeth's jian – a chinese double-edged straight sword

WOULD YOU TRUST THIS MAN?

When Sao Feng accuses Barbossa of treachery, he acts shocked. After all, Barbossa is an honest man!

SECRET SWORDS

Before Elizabeth can meet Sao Feng his guards demand that she remove her outergarments. She feigns outrage but the guards soon discover two swords concealed in the lining of her coat.

The Empress

Feared throughout the South China Seas, Sao Feng's pirate junk brings despair into the hearts of respectable merchants from the Gulf of Siam to Macao. Don't snigger at the word 'junk', the term is simply derived from the Malay word for boat, 'jong'. Far from being a product of the scrapyard, the junk is one of the most successful ship designs of all time, and has been gracing the water of the Orient since the second century AD.

Sails

The sails of a junk are not square-rigged as on most western sailing ships, but are positioned so that they can turn towards the wind, and sail almost straight into it. Slightly curved, the aerodynamic cut of the sails makes them similar to those used in modern-day windsurfing.

Fore mast

Main mast

Sails made from canvas matting

Mast made from oak

Bamboo supports (battens) strengthen sails and make them easier to roll up in high winds

Ship painted in bright colours

Anchor

Traditional painted eye for boat to 'see' with

Prisoners kept in cargo hold – some for too long...

FIRE POWER
The *Empress* carries 15 heavy iron cannons. As well as cannonballs, Sao Feng also likes to rely on the old Chinese practice of firing 'stink bombs' – clay pots loaded with gunpowder, nails and sulphur, plus any other nasty refinements his crew can add to the payload if they're in need of entertainment.

Stern section customised with
canvas structures that resemble
dragon wings

Mizen
mast

Sao Feng's
quarters

Captain's Quarters

Sao Feng's personal quarters
are lavishly decorated and
painted in exotic dyes to
emphasise his exalted position
on the ship. The adjustable
rudder is also controlled from
this stern section.

Gunpowder and
ball magazine

Crew's
quarters

Cannon

Hold can store over 600
tons of cargo, including
treasure chests, gunpowder
and weapons

Ballast (round rocks)
in bilges to help stop
the ship from capsizing
in high winds

Watertight
bulkheads

Ingenious Design

For centuries junks were the largest and safest ships in the world
due to a number of innovative features. Internal walls made the
structure of the junks extra rigid and created watertight
compartments (bulkheads) that could contain water in the case of a
leak. The flat-bottomed hull and an adjustable rudder that could be
raised or lowered, ensured that junks could sail on the ocean as well
as in more shallow waters like large rivers. The rudder itself was
located on the stern which made it easier to steer a straight course.

Captain's Cabin

Sao Feng agrees to help Barbossa and the crew escape Beckett and regain the *Black Pearl* – as long as Elizabeth joins him aboard his opulent junk the *Empress*. Will opposes this deal, but Elizabeth agrees in order to help her friends. Sao Feng has no scruples about now betraying Beckett. Feng is an honourable man – and he believes there is no honour in staying with the losing side...

COSY CABIN
Junks traditionally have comfortable quarters for a captain to house his wife or family in.

Joining the Winners

Lit by the warm glow of candle lanterns, the *Empress* welcomes back its captain after Sao Feng's raid on the *Black Pearl*. Joining the winners is just sound judgement according to Sao Feng. When Barbossa tells him that the pirates have Calypso on their side, the Pirate Lord of Singapore is happy to return to his old freebooting ways.

CAPTAIN'S TABLE
Exotic artifacts, from ancient acupuncture needles to fragrance burners, are among Sao Feng's most prized possessions. Many of them have been stolen at the cost of countless lives – but never his own. Remedies and elixirs to treat every pirate wound and want are found here.

Sao Feng performs ancient ritual to bring them good luck on their voyage.

Table draped in fine silk cloth embroidered with flowers. The peony represents spring.

Empress of the Empress

Sao Feng wastes no time in lavishing his attention and riches on his beautiful guest, selecting a magnificent traditional Chinese gown for Elizabeth. She wears the costume as if born to it, although she did need the help of three hand maidens to get into it. Hanging silks, soft pillows and candlelight create a romantic atmosphere, so it's not surprising that Sao Feng soon develops an urge to recite love poetry.

Ornate headdress

Silken tassels festoon the headdress

Priceless pearls and jade adorn the collar

FAVOUR OR FURY

Wine, fine words and a free outfit – not a bad start to her career as a pirate captive, admits Elizabeth. But sneaky Sao Feng confesses that if he cannot soon win her favour, he will be happy to accept her fury.

Gold thread

A TWIST OF FATE

Unfortunately for all aboard the *Empress,* Sao Feng's good luck ritual fails to work and the ship is attacked by the *Flying Dutchman.* In a split second everything changes and for Elizabeth, things take a new and surprising course.

Robe embroidered with traditional flowers and leaves

Luxurious silk cloth

Sao Feng's Map

Anyone planning that most difficult of voyages –
a trip to the Land Beyond Death, must first seek the
World's End. Only one map can take you there, Sao Feng's
navigational chart to the Farthest Gate. Its unique series
of rings means that locations are never fixed.
As Tai Huang points out – it may not
be as accurate as modern charts –
but it leads to more places.

*Red fabric
unraveled from
Sao Feng's ring*

THE GUARDIAN
Proud protector of this priceless
cartographical phenomenon,
Sao Feng does not keep it at
his waterfront lair – where the
damp salty air could damage
its delicate pigmentation. It
is closely guarded at a sacred
temple owned by his wise
and wizened old uncle.

*Sao Feng carries the
irreplaceable sea
charts on his back to
keep them safe
from harm.*

HERE BE DRAGONS
Strange symbols and images appear in the
mystical meanderings of this map's contours
– sometimes a dragon emerges, a harbinger
of great fortune in war. Traditional
navigators may founder, expecting the chart
to contain solid fact. They are missing the
point. Its very purpose is to lead sailors
astray – for only the truly lost can find a
place that cannot be reached.

RIDDLE IN THE MIDDLE

"Over the edge, back, over again, sunrise sets at the flash of green." This ancient riddle accompanies a central depiction of an intrepid junk. This picture, circled by a diagram of the phases of the moon, will point the way to the gate.

THE SEARCH FOR CAPTAIN JACK

If any man can return from Davey Jones' locker, it is the free-spirited Jack Sparrow, who never was one to treat anything in a straightforward way – especially death. Gibbs reveals that on rare occasions, at the last gleam of sunset, a green ray flashes up into the sky. Sailors believe this is a sign of a soul returning to our world from the dead.

FIERCE DEFENDER

When the tiger on this ring lines up with your destination, a safe passage is assured. At the time this map was created, this big cat was seen as a devourer of evil spirits and was believed to be a lucky omen.

Shipwreck Island

The bell has been raised from its watery grave, the nine pieces of eight are to be reunited and the Pirate Lords will meet at their legendary retreat. This is a stronghold so secret, so well defended, it can only be taken by treachery and betrayal – something pirates know a thing or two about. This is the hidden haunt that Lord Beckett is so desperate to discover, he's even prepared to trust Captain Jack Sparrow as his guide.

One vessel that has successfully navigated its way through The Devil's Throat

THE DEVIL'S THROAT

There's no shortage of quaintly carved wreckage to decorate the city. That's because the approach to Shipwreck Cove is through a perilous sea tunnel called The Devil's Throat, which claims several vessels each year.

Shipwreck City

Shipwreck City, in Shipwreck Cove, on Shipwreck Island proves one thing – that while pirates are clever clogs capable of the most ingenious evil schemes, they are an unimaginative lot when it comes to naming things. Once inside this rogues' refuge, however, you'll see plenty of evidence of their resourcefulness – in recycling other people's belongings. The whole place is built out of derelict and broken ships, and you'll find shops selling weapons, instruments and jewellery. It's a surprisingly homey hang-out with pirate urchins playing in the streets and hungry buccaneers building a home-made barbecue out of old torture equipment.

The Summons

With Beckett's Armada growing with each conquest and hapless pirates across the globe dancing the Hangman's Jig at his command, something drastic must be done. Barbossa sends forth the pirate song *Hoist the Colours* to summon pirates to Shipwreck Island, where they will decide what should be done about their common enemy:

"The bell has been raised from its watery grave,
Do you hear its sepulchral tone?
A call to all, pay heed the squall
And turn your sails toward home."

BRETHREN COURT

An abandoned hull forms the chamber of the Brethren Court. Surrounded by the curved spars of the wrecked ship sits an historic meeting table that has witnessed much pirate business and bloodshed, and it is around this table that the nine Pirate Lords once again convene.

Shipwreck City

Different kinds of pirate ships from all over the world are moored around the city

VOLCANIC CRATER

The island itself is a volcanic crater, its extinct cone providing the calm, circular haven of the fabled cove. There's no danger of the volcano erupting, but the pirates' tempers are another matter.

Pirate Lords

Timbers shiver across the world when these nine Buccaneers are assembled. Not mere pirates, these are all Lords – fabled captains with awesome ships, notorious crews and agreed territories. Gathered together, the Nine Lords once created the Pirate Code. The first time they met they captured the Sea Goddess Calypso, bound her in human shape, and tamed the sea for their own era of conquest. What this meeting has in store, none can yet guess...

Captain Jack Sparrow
None has travelled further than the Pirate Lord of the Caribbean to attend this shindig – back from Davy Jones' Locker.

Captain Barbossa
Lord of the Caspian Sea, this charming cut-throat called this meeting, because after years of mutual slaughter, the pirates are now united against a common enemy. Barbossa's message is clear, "Death to the East India Company!" His plan is to free Calypso in the hope that she will destroy Beckett and his fleet.

Gold-headed cane used by dignitaries

Frilly lace used to trim sleeves and to make cravat

Captain Sao Feng
The Pirate Lord of the South China Sea, Sao Feng, is a shrewd and powerful pirate. He commands the respect of pirates from across the globe and has well-trained warriors and a fleet of ships at his disposal.

Breeches

Barbossa's infamous pistol

Stockings

Capitaine Chevalle
Pirate Lord of the Mediterranean Sea, this faded flower of French aristocracy has now fallen on hard times. He likes to describe himself as penniless, but he is usually not short of a few gold doubloons.

LORDS OF THE GLOBE

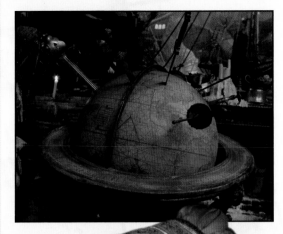

Before the Brethren Court can commence, each of the nine Pirate Lords is required by tradition to thrust a sword into a globe of the earth. This symbolises the pirates' right to plunder the world and also marks a desire to put away the sword while they are gathered together to Parlay. But while their swords may be out of action, this doesn't stop the Pirate Lords from carrying pistols, of course and it's rare for a session to pass without incident.

CAPTAIN VILLANUEVA

This taciturn Spaniard is Lord of the Adriatic. Unofficially retired, he is a realist who doubts that Calypso will ever forgive the brethren. Years of captivity will not have improved her mood, he observes.

Leather coat embossed with floral design

Silk headdress

AMMAND THE CORSAIR

The Pirate Lord of the Black Sea is known as the Scourge of the Barbary Coast. An expert in the art of galley warfare, he is swift to strike, a master of escape and immensely proud of his moustache.

GENTLEMAN JOCARD

Terror of the Atlantic, Jocard was a slave who rose by cunning, charm and casual slaughter to the heights of Pirate Lord. He mistrusts Calypso and suggests cutting out Barbossa's tongue.

Woollen cloak from Morocco

Fashionable wide moustache

Dragon motif adorns silk robe

Opal and gold clasp fastens on turban

Traditional tribal costume

MISTRESS CHING

Pirate Lord of the Pacific Ocean, this ruthless Chinese pirate commands a massive fleet of pirate junks. Mistress Ching knows better than most how to weigh a man's words, and scorns Barbossa's fancy speechifying.

SRI SUMBHAJEE

This serene and priestly Hindu is Pirate Lord of the Indian Ocean. Opposed to the East India Company and Calypso, he is also against the outdated laws of the Pirate Code. He's as deep as the ocean depths he sends his enemies down to.

Curled-toe slippers

The Wrath of Calypso

The time for Parlay is over and the pirates and the East India Trading Company are now at war. Far out at sea, the ships of the nine Pirate Lords face Lord Beckett's fleet of over three hundred vessels. Not exactly a fair fight, some might say, but then there is Calypso. The Goddess of the Sea has yet to play her part in the day's drama. The sky darkens, the clouds rotate with unnatural speed, and the sea begins to churn in an ever-widening circle, becoming an immense whirlpool. The Maelstrom has been unleashed...

The Flying Dutchman *leads the East India Company onslaught*

The Dutchman *is drawn towards the fast inner circles of the whirlpool*

Galleons, ketches, sloops, schooners, galleys and junks – the battle brings together the great ships of the age of piracy

When the pirates release Calypso from her human bonds, a bolt of lightning strikes the sea and a giant whirlpool is formed

The Black Pearl *leads the pirates – she's the only ship fast enough to catch the* Flying Dutchman

Battle in the Maelstrom

As Calypso vents her fury the *Black Pearl* and *Flying Dutchman* are drawn into the Maelstrom. Amidst the crashes of thunder and the roar of the sea, the sound of cannon fire can be heard as the two infamous ships battle across the abyss.

Index

LONDON, NEW YORK, MUNICH,
MELBOURNE AND DELHI

Senior Editor Lindsay Kent   **Project Designer** Lisa Crowe
Publishing Manager Simon Beecroft   **Designer** Cathy Tincknell
Category Publisher Alex Allan   **Brand Manager** Lisa Lanzarini
Production Rochelle Talary   **DTP Design** Lauren Egan & Hanna Ländin

First published in Great Britain in 2006
This revised edition published in 2007 by
Dorling Kindersley Limited,
80 Strand, London WC2R 0RL
A Penguin Company

2 4 6 8 10 9 7 5 3 1
PD202 – 01/07

Pirates of the Caribbean: The Curse of the Black Pearl, Pirates of the Caribbean: Dead Man's Chest and *Pirates
of the Caribbean: At World's End*
Based on the screenplay written by Ted Elliott & Terry Rossio
Based on characters created by Ted Elliott & Terry Rossio and Stuart Beattie and Jay Wolpert
Based on Walt Disney's Pirates of the Caribbean
Produced by Jerry Bruckheimer
Directed by Gore Verbinski

A CIP catalogue record for this book is available from the British Library.

ISBN: 978-1-40532-006-1

Reproduced by Media Development and Printing Ltd., UK
Printed and bound in China by Leo Paper Products, Ltd.

Acknowledgements

The publisher would like to thank the following for their kind permission to reproduce their illustrations:
(key: a-above; c-centre; b-below; l-left; r-right; t-top)
Richard Bonson 30–31; Mauro Borrelli 3r, 63r, 64–65 main illustration, 64t, 65t, 65c, 65b;
James Carson 52–53, 63l; Diane Chadwick 46–47; Crash McCreery 62, 64bl, 73br;
Robert Nelmes 8–9, 72–73; Nathan Schroeder 56–57.

The Publisher would also like to thank the following people:
Jerry Bruckheimer for kindly writing the foreword; Mary Mullen, Jon Rogers, Rich Thomas, Graham Barnard and
Lisa Gerstel at Disney for all their help; Rick Heinrichs, Carla Nemec, Sarah Contant and Megan Romero at Second
Mate Producions for their hospitality and invaluable help.

Discover more at
www.dk.com